Systematic Analysis of University Libraries:

An Application of Cost-Benefit Analysis to the M.I.T. Libraries

Systematic Analysis of University Libraries:

An Application of Cost-Benefit Analysis to the M.I.T. Libraries

Jeffrey A. Raffel
Robert Shishko

THE M.I.T. PRESS
Cambridge, Massachusetts, and London, England

Contents

List of Figures   vii

List of Tables   ix

Foreword by Fred Charles Iklé   xi

Acknowledgments   xv

Introduction   1

1: The Program Budget   3

    A Program Budget for the M.I.T. Libraries   3
    Implications of the Program Budget   6

2: Storing the Collection   7

    Modeling Book Storage Costs   7
    Implications of Storage Costs   14
    An Example of an Inexpensive Storage System   15
    Bringing Inexpensively Stored Books to the User:
      Retrieval Systems   19
    Microform Storage   21
    Storage of Books: Conclusion   22

3: Providing Study Spaces and Required Reading Material   23

    Introduction   23
    The Present Study-Reserve System   24
    Alternative Study-Reserve Systems   24
    Study-Reserve Alternatives: Conclusion   29
    Suboptimizing Seating Accommodations in the Library   29

4: Fulfilling Research Requirements   35

    Introduction   35
    Alternative Cataloging Schemes   36
    An Analysis of Temporary Cataloging   37

Alternative Ordering Schemes   39
Extra-M.I.T. Retrieval Systems   40
Access to Other Collections   40
Improved Selection and Acquisition   41
Comparing Alternative Selection Plans   43
Common Acquisition with Wellesley   45

5: Benefit Evaluation   46

Desirable Characteristics of Benefit Measures   46
Measuring Benefits by Survey Research Procedures   48
Problems and Limitations of Surveying Benefits   49
Results: Absolute Preference   58
Results: Response Patterns   61
Results: Subgroup Analysis   63
Conclusion   67

6: Conclusions   68

Major Findings   68
Future Research Questions   72

Appendix 1:   Personnel Time Study   75
Appendix 2:   Program Budget—1966 to 1967   78
Appendix 3:   Floor Space in Square Feet   80
Appendix 4:   Cost Per Item—From M.I.T. Program Budget   81
Appendix 5:   Average Storage Costs   82
Appendix 6:   Data for Criteria Comparison   84
Appendix 7:   Projected Students and Faculty at M.I.T.   86
Appendix 8:   Departmental Library Alternatives   87
Appendix 9:   Study-Reserve Alternatives   88
Appendix 10: Number and Price of U.S. Serials and
                 Periodicals by Category Projected
                 Through 1976   90
Appendix 11: Duplicating Catalogs on Microform   93
Appendix 12: Number and Price of U.S. Hardcover and
                 Paperback Books by Category Projected
                 Through 1976   94
Appendix 13: Systems by Cost and Preference Ranks   99
Appendix 14: Association Between System Pairs   100

Bibliography   103

Index   105

List of Figures

Figure

1 Breakdown of library budget by program. Total budget $2,280,000.   4

2 Breakdown of general and research collection budget. Total budget $1,677,000.   5

3 Breakdown of required reading and studying budget. Total budget $528,000.   5

4 Stacks floor-plan model.   8

5 Average 1966 circulation of a book as a function of x, the number of years since its publication.   16

6 Percent circulation "lost" vs. percent books removed.   16

7 Comparison of total cost for two storage alternatives.   20

8 All Library of Congress cataloging including Title II C through 1990.   37

9 M.I.T. materials appropriations projected through 1974.   39

10 List price index of books (hardcover, trade-technical) projected through 1976 (1957–1959 = 100.0).   42

11 M.I.T. and Wellesley annual acquisitions projected through 1976. 43

12 Benefit survey.   50

13 Association among "outside-use orientation" systems.   62

14 Association among "research orientation" systems.   62

15 Projected student enrollment at M.I.T.   86

16 Projected faculty at M.I.T.   86

17 Growth in U.S. serials and periodicals by category projected through 1976.   90

18 Average price of U.S. periodicals projected through 1976.   91

19 Growth of U.S. serials and periodicals in the natural sciences and engineering projected through 1976.   91

20 Growth of U.S. periodicals and serials in the social sciences projected through 1976.   92

21 Average price of U.S. periodicals by category projected through 1976.   92

22 Annual number of new nonfiction titles and editions including imports (as listed in *Publishers' Weekly*) available in the U.S. projected through 1974.   94

Figure

23   Annual number of new U.S. hardcover nonfiction titles and edi-   94
     tions (as listed in *Publishers' Weekly*) projected through 1974.
24   Annual number of new U.S. hardcover and paperback titles and   95
     editions (as listed in *Publishers' Weekly*) projected through 1974.
25   Average list price of U.S. published trade paperback books pro-   95
     jected through 1976.
26   Average list price of U.S. published hardcover, trade-technical   96
     books projected through 1976.
27   Average list price of U.S. published science and engineering   96
     books projected through 1976.
28   Average list price of U.S. published social science books pro-   97
     jected through 1976.

List of Tables

Table

1	Square Feet of Stacks per Section	8
2	Access Requirements	9
3	Volumes per Single-Faced Section	9
4	Alternative Compacting Plans	10
5	Estimated Maintenance Costs	11
6	Estimated Construction Costs	11
7	Cost/Volume Associated with Various Storage Alternatives	13
8	Factors Making up Volume Equivalents	14
9	Annual Savings for Alternative Weeding Criteria	18
10	Comparative Seating Costs	28
11	Summary of Reserve-Study Alternatives	30
12	Seating Statistics for Large University Libraries	33
13	Systems Relating to Research Needs	35
14	Cataloging Costs by Activity and Personnel	36
15	Number of New Editions and Titles Published from 1962 and Projected through 1976	42
16	Hypothetical Output Levels Associated with Varying Selection Inputs	44
17	Preference Rankings by Budget Levels	57
18	Percentage of Respondents Choosing System by Budget Level	58
19	System Preferences by M.I.T. Status at $200,000 Budget Level	63
20	System Preferences by M.I.T. Status at $0 Budget Level	64
21	Field by Preferences at the $200,000 Budget Level	66
22	Main Purpose of Library to Respondents	66
23	Perceived Purposes of Library by Preferences at $200,000 Budget Level	67

Foreword

Fred Charles Iklé

As the administrators and librarians on every campus know, limited resources force hard choices among many desirable schemes for expanding and improving library facilities. What percentage of new books should be acquired, how much service should be provided, how luxurious or austere should new library buildings be?

An allocation of resources involves—either implicitly or explicitly—a comparison of alternatives. The more explicit, the more coherent, the more "rational" this comparison is to be, the more difficult the task. The difficulties of analysis have many sources: A policy (or *system*) frequently serves several objectives; the future environment is always uncertain; and the costs and benefits of alternative policies (*systems*) are difficult to predict and hard to measure.

Such allocation problems have, of course, been dealt with in a rather systematic fashion for many decades, primarily by economists specializing in public finance and by administrators and civil engineers concerned with public works.[1] Initially, this was done in the water resources area,[2] then for the allocation of military budgets,[3] and more recently for a wide variety of public issues.[4] During the last ten years, a methodology has been developed for the sort of

[1]An early treatise is Eugene L. Grant and W. Grant Jerson, *Principles of Engineering Economy* (New York: The Ronald Press Company, 1964). First edition in 1930.

[2]Roland N. McKean, *Efficiency in Government through Systems Analysis: With Emphasis on Water Resources Development* (New York: John Wiley & Sons, 1958).

[3]Charles Hitch and Roland N. McKean, *The Economics of Defense in the Nuclear Age* (Cambridge, Mass.: Harvard University Press, 1960); E. S. Quade (ed.), *Analysis for Military Decisions* (Chicago: Rand-McNally, 1965).

[4]David Novick (ed.), *Program Budgeting* (Cambridge, Mass.: Harvard University Press, 1965); Robert Dorfman (ed.), *Measuring Benefits of Government Investments* (Washington, D.C.: The Brookings Institution, 1965).

analysis that looks at policy making as a choice among alternative systems.

To my knowledge, the present study by Jeffrey Raffel and Robert Shishko is the first application of this methodology to a university library. With some minor changes, their approach could be used for any library serving a limited or general public.

The Center for International Studies at M.I.T. (with the unstinting support of M.I.T.'s Director of Libraries) sponsored this study for two reasons. First, the M.I.T. libraries—like any other university library system—have to face difficult new demands while available resources, as a result of the general financial difficulties of American universities, become more restricted. A growing student enrollment, a constantly expanding volume of publications (12,000 new nonfiction titles in the United States in 1958, rising to perhaps 40,000 by 1972), and a shortage of real estate and building funds constitute the more traditional problems for those responsible for library planning. New problems, and at the same time new opportunities, arise from the advances in library technology, such as various versions of the computerized catalog, automated bibliographic services, and quick facsimile reproduction.[5]

The second reason why this study is being published under sponsorship of the Center for International Studies is its didactic usefulness. Political Science, Economics, and other departments at M.I.T. seek to train students in the methods of systematic policy analysis (cost-benefit analysis), and the Center has a research program in support of this effort.

To teach this methodology, case studies seem essential. Yet, the difficulty with many cases dealing with actual government programs is that the student has to spend a lot of time familiarizing himself with the subject matter. In particular, the important tasks of problem formulation and systems delineation have to be simplified grossly for almost any government policy issue. The library system on campus is an ideal subject on which to practice the art of systems analysis. The students, being familiar with the larger context, can delineate the problem realistically. They can intelligently grapple with the formulation of benefit criteria since they have experienced the benefits, or lack of them, themselves. And they can

[5]The Center for International Studies is participating in an effort to improve the M.I.T. libraries in the field of international relations and foreign economic development. This was the context in which the present study originated.

constructively invent new means and revise the formulation of ends on the basis of this familiarity.

The present study leaves ample room for further research; it does not pre-empt the subject. A real-life systems analysis never reaches a clear-cut stage where it can be said to be completed. The uncertainties of future technology should receive more attention in a follow-on study to this one, and additional sensitivity tests would strengthen the findings. Furthermore, more work could usefully be done on the measurement of benefits (as in nearly every systems analysis!). Another extension of considerable methodological interest would be an exploration of higher levels of optimization. For instance, the preferred library system might differ if the resources to be allocated to it were not just the library expenditures of the university as a corporation but the sum of expenditures on books and related library matters by the corporation, the faculty, and the students. The present study offers some interesting statistics on this point. Another expansion (i.e., higher level optimization) would be a combined analysis of library *and* teaching facilities.

For those not familiar with the limitation of this kind of systematic policy analysis, a word of caution might be in order. The analysis begins with the computation of a program budget, i.e., a budget that combines the usual librarian's budget for books and personnel with the university expenditures (or opportunity costs) for library buildings. To our knowledge, such a program budget has rarely, if ever, been computed for a university library. But such a presentation of the budget might seem undesirable to those who have to bargain for more money within the bureaucracy of a university. The chief librarian wants more money for books and staff, and he might fear that if the university capital budget saved money because a systems analyst recommended a trade-off of stack space for more books, he, the librarian, might lose the stack space but never obtain the additional budget for books.

At the level of the university comptroller or president, the same kind of bureaucratic constraints might come into conflict with the rationale of a systems analysis. Not all the monies used for library purposes are fungible. A private donation, for instance, might be earmarked for a library *building*, so that the opportunity cost of this building ought to be calculated at less than construction cost, or even at zero, depending on the flexibilities in other budget accounts. Likewise, federal assistance might be earmarked for the acquisition of books only, for microfilming, or for a computerized catalog, rather than for the university library system as a whole.

A good systems analyst is, of course, quite aware of institutional constraints that inhibit the reallocation of resources. His analysis can either incorporate these constraints as given constants or treat them as variables subject to improvements. Bureaucratic rules, after all, are proper candidates for reform.

Acknowledgments

We would primarily like to thank Professor Fred Charles Iklé for suggesting that we analyze the M.I.T. libraries in the cost-benefit framework. Professor Iklé has helped us to realize that systematic analysis can be a powerful aid in evaluating alternative allocations of resources. At the same time, he has helped us appreciate some of the pitfalls inherent in this approach to decision making. In addition, Professor Iklé was kind enough to assist in the arrangements for this study; his continuing interest and his ideas were crucial to any success we might have had.

We would also like to extend our sincere appreciation to Professor William N. Locke, Director of the M.I.T. libraries, and Miss Natalie N. Nicholson, Assistant Director of the M.I.T. libraries. Both gave freely of their time and assistance to introduce us to the complexities of the operations of the M.I.T. libraries. Their questions, criticisms, and suggestions served to focus our attention on the key issues before library decision-makers. We thank them for their aid and hope our work will prove as beneficial to them as their aid was to us.

It is impossible to thank properly all the library staff who cooperated with us by completing surveys and questionnaires, searching obscure file cabinets, and explaining the nature of their work to two querelous investigators. We would like to single out, however, Miss Frances R. Lubovitz, Director of the Cataloging Department, and Miss Barbara Klingenhagen, Director of the Dewey Library, for their special efforts in providing us with the information and data we required.

The Center for International Studies at M.I.T. deserves special credit for venturing outside of more limited concerns to sponsor and finance this study. We appreciate their sponsorship and hope our study will be of value to them. The M.I.T. Libraries also helped finance this study and again we must extend our appreciation.

The abundance of graphs, tables, figures, and words would have disturbed a less talented and patient editor than Miss Nancy Poling at the Center for International Studies. She was faced with the tasks that we were unable to do ourselves. If any errors are found in syntax or typing, we must blame ourselves and thank Miss Poling for the scores she found when we did not. Further thanks are due Mrs. Jennifer Thompson for her typing of early drafts of the manuscript.

Mr. Shishko would like to thank Professor W. W. Kaufmann of the M.I.T. Department of Political Science for introducing him to the wide range of applications of systematic analysis and for encouraging him to pursue cost-benefit analysis as a profession.

Mr. Raffel would also like to thank two former teachers who had an indirect but strong influence on the effort. Dr. Gerald Kramer introduced him to decision analysis and Dr. Hanan Selvin to survey analysis and methodology at the University of Rochester. He hopes that this book will provide them with the rewards of teaching as their lectures and personal interest provided the rewards of learning. Mr. Raffel thanks his patient wife, Joanne, for incurring the costs of her husband's work and long hours away while he gained the benefits of a task completed. He hopes that the benefits will be distributed more equitably in the future.

Cambridge, Massachusetts   JEFFREY RAFFEL
New Haven, Connecticut   ROBERT SHISHKO
April 1969

Introduction

The natural starting point for any cost-benefit study is a formulation of the problem and a structuring of the analysis. The way in which the problem is formulated is important for at least two reasons: First, it sets the limitations of the study by isolating those aspects of the problem that will be investigated and those alternatives that will be considered; and second, it determines whether or not the study is, in fact, systematic.

The techniques of systems analysis suggest that one begin this study by identifying missions of the library. Identifying missions is by no means an easy task, since one can easily be led down the wrong road by confusing *past output*, i.e., performance, with *desired output*, i.e., objectives. The difficulties do not end there, since different libraries usually find it desirable (or necessary) to emphasize different missions, depending upon the nature of the parent organization.

The planned library at the new Federal City College in Washington, D.C., provides an interesting example. One could easily suggest that the mission of this library is "to stimulate the desire to learn." To this end, the library facility has been designed to lure students rather than intimidate them. Some of the innovations that are planned include (a) carpeted lounging areas in between the cafeteria and the library for students to have snacks, talk, play records, and browse through periodicals, (b) carrels with built-in tape and phone equipment, and (c) a bookstore serving as a "direct extension" of the library that may serve free coffee and pastry and provide lounging and reading areas complete with FM music.

While it seems that the designers of the Federal City College Library had explicitly in mind objectives such as "to encourage the use of library materials" and "to provide the appropriate atmosphere for informal discussions," other libraries may not see these as primary objectives.

1

We have identified at least two principal missions for the M.I.T. library system. The first is to provide material for students' course work: their assigned reading as well as reference and background reading for essays, term papers, and research projects. There are several subsidiary objectives relating to this mission:
1. To select, acquire, and organize material for course-related work;
2. To make this material available to users;
3. To provide reference and bibliographic information; and
4. To provide facilities for studying course-related material.

The second principal mission is to provide material in general support of research at M.I.T. Again there are several subsidiary objectives relating to this mission:
1. To select, acquire, and organize material for research;
2. To make this material available to users;
3. To provide search and bibliographic aids; and
4. To provide facilities for research where desirable.

The present state of the library system at M.I.T. reflects the general preponderance of science, engineering, and social science, but in the future the library may reflect a whole range of intellectual concerns of which science and technology are but a part. The problem is how to organize future library resources into a set of programs that best fulfill these objectives.

1 The Program Budget

A Program Budget for the M.I.T. Libraries

The first task was to translate the current library budget into a budget relating outputs to inputs, i.e., a program budget. This allows the analyst to disaggregate and reaggregate relevant costs and to expand the reporting of costs to include overhead, fringe benefits, general administration, and other quasi-fixed costs. These costs are a part of M.I.T.'s expenses in maintaining the libraries but are not charged directly to the M.I.T. library budget.

The program budget was disaggregated to display those categories (i.e., activities) for which the library was already noting output statistics. Personnel costs, in both the Central Processing and Handling Services, and in the divisional libraries (Dewey, Hayden) were determined by multiplying the average salaries, fringe benefits, and general administration costs[1] associated with library personnel at various professional levels by the percentage of time such personnel reported spending on each of the program budget activities (Appendix 1). These time reports were taken in a July time survey which covered only the Student Center, Dewey, and the Humanities libraries, and the cataloging, acquisitions, and circulation departments. About three-quarters (73%) of those responding stated that the time allocation reported for the previous day's work was "very typical" or "typical" for their work during the summer.[2]

Floor-space costs included a charge of $1.25 per square foot for general maintenance and $2.54 per square foot as a uniform annual repayment of the capital costs and interest charges on the capital costs.

[1]Fringe benefit and general administration (payroll, hiring, etc.) were reported by the Comptroller's Office to add 28.5% to actual salary figures.

[2]A further survey is necessary to indicate the reliability of the summer survey. The reliability appears to be lowest where the categories include the fewest number of workers and, fortunately, the least expense.

Maintenance costs were provided by the Superintendent's Office. These figures included lighting, heating, water, cleaning, guards, and supervision.

Capital costs were estimated at $40 per gross square foot for an air-conditioned, on-campus library or storage facility. We used an interest rate of 6.0%, and costs were allocated over a 50-year repayment period.[3] A more detailed discussion of the treatment of capital costs can be found in the report on alternative storage arrangements (Chapter 2).

Jobber and supply costs were reported by library administrators. Supply costs in the cataloging department were accurately known,

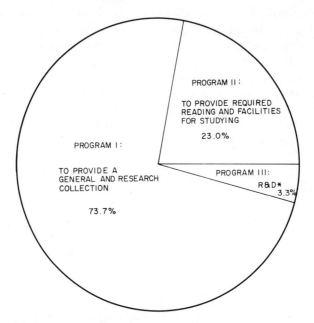

Figure 1. Breakdown of library budget by program.
Total budget $2,280,000.*

*Technical Information Processing Project, T.I.P.

[3]The following matrix illustrates the sensitivity of the uniform annual capital cost to variations in interest rate and construction costs:

$/Gross Ft^2	5.0%	5.5%	6.0%	6.5%	7.0%
35	$1.92	$2.07	$2.22	$2.38	$2.54
40	$2.19	$2.36	$2.54	$2.72	$2.90
45	$2.46	$2.66	$2.85	$3.06	$3.26
50	$2.74	$2.95	$3.17	$3.40	$3.62

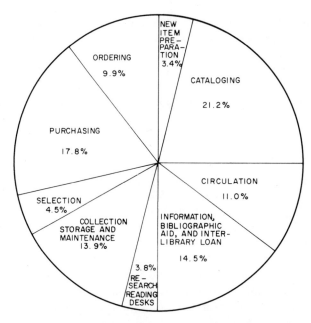

Figure 2. Breakdown of general and research collection budget. Total budget $1,677.000.

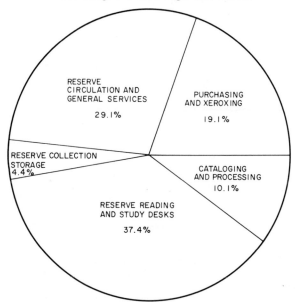

Figure 3. Breakdown of required reading and studying budget. Total budget $528,000.

but supply costs in the other functional categories were estimated. Fortunately, cataloging accounts for about 60% of the supply costs.

Output statistics were, in most cases, already available from the divisional libraries and central processing departmental annual reports. One important figure—the total number of inquiries in the information services—was estimated from a survey in the Hayden library.

Implications of the Program Budget

Figures 1, 2, and 3 show current expenditures by program category. (Appendix 2 gives a more detailed breakdown of the program budget; Appendix 3 gives the breakdown of the floor space in square feet; and Appendix 4 reports the cost per item in various categories.) Thus note that the M.I.T. libraries spend as much cataloging items as purchasing them, and that the libraries spend more to "store" people in study spaces (11.4%) than to store books in stacks (6.4%).

It is now possible to compare existing and new alternatives within each of the main program categories, and to identify trade-offs between program activities.

2   Storing the Collection

Modeling Book Storage Costs

The variables that the library can control in determining book storage policy are:

1. Location of the storage facility—on or off campus.
2. Type of storage—conventional (with room for expansion throughout) or compact (books shelved chronologically and by size).
3. Degree of user acess to the collection (closed or open stacks).

It is assumed that the degree of use associated with a given collection is a function of the type and size of the collection and the characteristics of those who use it. Although the nature of studying and research may change in future years, it was assumed that large-scale inexpensive storage alternatives at M.I.T. fall into the moderate-use category. The storage model used here, derived in part from the work of Metcalf,[1] estimates the number of square feet required to store an average book given the storage policy specifications. The basic variables of the model are aisle width (greatest where user traffic is greatest), range or individual stack length (longest where use is least), and stack capacity. Thus where stack use is heavy, necessitating more space for access, the total square feet required to store the books is greater.

Determining the Area Required per Section of Stacks

Sections are defined as 3 linear feet of single-faced shelves, 7-1/2 feet high. In our model, the following variables are necessary:

Let a be the aisle width in feet,

b be the cross aisle width in feet,

R be the range length in feet, and

S be the single shelf depth = 2/3 ft.

Figure 4 is included to make these definitions more meaningful.

[1] Keyes D. Metcalf, *Planning Academic and Research Library Buildings* (New York: McGraw-Hill Book Company, Inc., 1965).

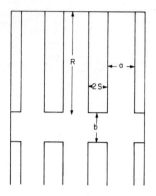

Figure 4.   Stacks floor-
plan model.

When there are many sections, the required area for each range
length is

$$A = (R + b)(a + 2S) \qquad (1)$$

Since each range length includes $R/3$ sections, and each range
length consists of double-faced shelves, there are $2/3\ R$ sections in
each range length. Then:

$$\frac{\text{sections}}{\text{ft}^2 \text{ of stacks}} = \frac{2/3\ R}{(R + b)(a + 4/3)} \qquad (2)$$

Table 1 gives the results of inserting $b = 3$ ft into Equation 2 for
various combinations of values for a and R.

Table 1   Square Feet of Stacks per Section

Aisle Width, a	Range Length, R						
	15 ft.	25 ft.	35 ft.	45 ft.	55 ft.	65 ft.	75 ft.
24 in.	6.0	5.6	5.4	5.3	5.3	5.2	5.2
26 in.	6.3	5.9	5.7	5.6	5.5	5.5	5.5
28 in.	6.6	6.2	6.0	5.9	5.8	5.8	5.7
30 in.	6.9	6.4	6.3	6.1	6.1	6.0	6.0
32 in.	7.2	6.7	6.5	6.4	6.3	6.3	6.2
34 in.	7.5	7.0	6.8	6.7	6.6	6.6	6.5
36 in.	7.8	7.3	7.0	6.9	6.9	6.8	6.8
38 in.	8.1	7.6	7.3	7.2	7.1	7.1	7.0
40 in.	8.4	7.9	7.6	7.5	7.4	7.4	7.3
42 in.	8.7	8.1	7.9	7.8	7.7	7.6	7.6

The entries that have been boxed in indicate those combinations that Metcalf considers feasible. From Equation 2, it can be seen that the number of square feet per section is not a function of the location of the storage facility or of the type of storage, i.e., conventional, compact. The required area is a function only of the degree of expected use and the type of access, i.e., closed or open.

For a college research library, in particular the M.I.T. library system, only the alternatives listed in Table 2 were considered relevant.

Table 2.   Access Requirements

Access	Degree of Expected Use	Ft²/Section
Open	Heavy	7.8
Open	Moderate	7.0
Open	Infrequent	6.4
Closed	Moderate	6.4
Closed	Infrequent	5.9

Determining the Number of Volumes per Section

For conventional storage we can refer again to Metcalf, who estimates the average number of volumes that could be stored on a single-faced section of stacks.[2] (See Table 3.) The choice of a single number depends on a number of assumptions about the composition of the collection. A figure of 125 vol./sec was chosen since this figure is considered the standard number of books that can be stored in a section when one-third of that section is left empty for expansion of the collection.

Table 3.   Volumes per Single-Faced Section

Fiction	168
Circulating nonfiction	168
Economics	168
General literature	147
History	147
Art	147
Technical and scientific	126
Public documents	105
Bound periodicals	105

Compact storage: Metcalf discusses various methods of compacting. The Yale Compact Storage Study, a part of Yale's Selective Book Retirement Program, shows that the added cost of mechanical

[2]*Ibid.*, p. 393.

and mobile shelving offsets any gain in the utilization of space.
Table 4 shows the effect of three alternative compacting plans. In
combination, the gain in the utilization of space is greater than the
"sum of its parts."

Table 4.   Alternative Compacting Plans

Method of Compacting	Percentage Increase in Vol./Section	Vol./Section
Size (five groups)	20%	150
Chronological	32%	165
Fore-edge	35%	169
Combination	95%	244

Storing books chronologically means that no space is left for
expansion of the collection as in conventional storage.

The number of volumes per square foot of stacks is then simply
given by:

$$\frac{\text{vol.}}{\text{ft}^2} = \frac{\text{vol./section}}{\text{ft}^2/\text{section}} \qquad (3)$$

Determination of Unusable Area Factor

The unusable area factor (UAF) denotes space devoted to stair-
ways, restrooms, entrances, etc., all of which must be a part of any
storage facility. The factor depends basically on the expected degree
of use and the size of the facility. Hence we have employed the
following scheme to obtain the UAF:

Degree of Use	Unusable Area Factor
Heavily used	1.25
Moderately used	1.20
Infrequently used	1.15

The ft²/volume figure is then multiplied by the UAF to obtain the
gross ft²/volume, which of course is the figure used in computing
building and maintenance costs.

Maintenance Costs

Table 5 shows the maintenance costs estimated by the Superintendent's Office. These figures include lighting, heating, power,

water, cleaning, guards, and supervision. The annual maintenance cost per volume stored is obtained by multiplying these maintenance costs by the gross area per volume.

Table 5.   Estimated Maintenance Costs

1. On-campus library maintenance for a heavily used facility	$1.50/yr-ft^2
2. On-campus library maintenance for a moderately used facility	$1.25/yr-ft^2
3. On-campus storage facility for infrequently used material	$ .90/yr-ft^2
4. On-campus heavily used (open 24 hr per day) study facility such as the Student Center Library	$2.50/yr-ft^2
5. Off-campus moderately used library (i.e., same as on-campus)	$1.25/yr-ft^2
6. Off-campus storage facility	$ .90/yr-ft^2
7. Off-campus storage warehouse, such as the New England Depository Library	$ .60/yr-ft^2

Building and Land Costs

Construction costs were estimated by the M.I.T. Operations Office. Based on recent construction at M.I.T., the figures from Table 6 were used.

Table 6.   Estimated Construction Costs

Buildings	
On-campus library and/or storage facility (air-conditioned)	$38/gross-ft^2
Off-campus library and/or storage facility (air-conditioned)	$33/gross-ft^2
Off-campus storage warehouse (air-conditioned)	$25/gross-ft^2
Land	
On-campus or nearby real estate	$12/gross-ft^2
Off-campus real estate	$ 3/gross-ft^2

The amount of land required for a building, of course, depends on the architecture, number of floors, landscaping, parking facilities, etc. For on-campus buildings, we have assumed a building of four floors plus a basement similar to the Hermann Building with no new parking facilities. For off-campus buildings, we have again assumed a building of four floors plus a basement, but with parking facilities depending on the expected degree of use. The final cost figures are not sensitive to any of these assumptions.

Once the capital expenditure figures were determined, they were transformed by Equation 4 into a *uniform annual* cost that includes repayment of the principal and interest on the unpaid portion of it over the entire life of the system. Land, naturally, was not amortized; only the interest on the cost of the land was counted.

$$R = P \left[\frac{i(1 + i)^n}{(1 + i)^n - 1} \right] = P(\text{c.r.f.}) \qquad (4)$$

where R is the uniform annual capital cost, P is the principal, i is the interest rate, n is the repayment period, and c.r.f. is the capital recovery factor.

We have used an annual interest rate of 6% and a repayment period of $n = 50$ years. Provided n is "large," R is insensitive to changes in n.

Storage Equipment Costs

From the Yale study of book storage,[3] the cost of conventional shelving was found to be about $4/ft^2 of stacks while compact shelving was found to be about $6/ft^2 of stacks.

To convert these to uniform annual costs per volume, we assumed the same capital recovery factor. Thus

$$\frac{\text{storage equipment cost}}{\text{vol. yr}} = \frac{\text{storage equipment cost}}{\text{ft}^2 \text{ of stacks}} \times \frac{\text{ft}^2 \text{ of stacks}}{\text{vol.}}$$
$$\times \; [\text{c.r.f.} \; (i = 6\%; n = 50)] \qquad (5)$$

Total Cost Function

The total cost per volume per year is then the sum of the annual maintenance cost per volume, the uniform annual building and storage equipment cost per volume, and the annual interest charges on the cost of lands used for book storage per volume.

Table 7 summarizes our findings on costs and benefits of alternative book storage systems, and Appendix 5 gives a more detailed description of the cost data for each of the alternatives. The column on benefit considerations has been included to aid nonlibrarians in translating the technical descriptions of storage alternatives into user-oriented terms.

---

[3]See Lee Ash, *Yale's Selective Book Retirement Program* (New York: Shoe String Press, 1963).

Table 7.   Cost/Volume Associated with Various Storage Alternatives

Storage Alternative	Benefits	Cost/Vol./Yr
Infrequent use:		
(1) Open access, conventional storage, on campus	Browsing possible.	$ .2269
(2) Open access, conventional storage, off campus	Browsing possible only for those willing or able to travel off campus (presumably for special projects or papers). Retrieval system necessary, with delay incurred.	.1992
(3) Closed access, compact storage, off campus	Browsing impossible. Retrieval system necessary, with delay incurred.	.0752
Moderate use:		
(1) Open access, conventional storage, on campus	Browsing possible.	.2825
(2) Closed access, conventional storage, on campus	Browsing possible but discouraged except for special projects.	.2581
(3) Open access, conventional storage, off campus	Browsing possible for those willing to travel off campus. Retrieval system necessary, with delay incurred.	.2509
(4) Closed access, conventional storage, off campus	Browsing possible only under very special circumstances. Retrieval system necessary, with delay incurred.	.2293
(5) Closed access, compact storage, on campus	Browsing impossible but retrieval delay short.	.1360
(6) Closed access, compact storage, off campus	Browsing impossible, retrieval necessary, with delay incurred.	.1213
Heavy use:		
(1) Open access, conventional storage, on campus	Easy browsing possible.	.3474

Implications of Storage Costs

Standardization of the Collection

Our first step in analyzing overall storage costs was to standardize the M.I.T. collection, consisting of books, pamphlets, journals, serials, theses, and technical reports, to a base of 125 volumes per section used in the storage model. Table 8 displays the factors we used in translating these diversified types of material into *volume equivalents*.[4] In applying these factors to M.I.T.'s collection, a figure of 510,000 *volume equivalents* is obtained.

Table 8.   Factors Making up Volume Equivalents

1 volume equivalent	= 2/3 journals
	= 1 hardcover monograph
	= 4 serials
	= 2 theses
	= 2 technical reports
	= 4 pamphlets

Total Cost Comparisons for Alternative Storage Systems

Given our assumptions, we estimate the annual cost of leaving the collection open to browsing is ($.2825 − $.2581) $.0244 per volume equivalent. This figure is obtained by subtracting the annual cost of storing a volume equivalent on campus in a *closed*, conventional mode ($.2581) from the annual cost of storing a volume equivalent on campus in an *open*, conventional mode ($.2825). In terms of a total annual figure, the cost is about ($.0244 × 510,000) $12,500. Given a doubling of the collection in eight years, the saving resulting from closing the collection would then be about $25,000 per year.

Closing access to the collection may result in increased circulation costs as users call for books from storage which they would reject were browsing possible. Furthermore, benefits may be lost because difficulty in using the retrieval system may discourage some people from calling for marginally useful books.

A much larger total cost differential occurs when books are stored compactly, i.e., by size, and tightly packed. Such a compact storage system would naturally have to be a closed-access system since books are stored by size rather than subject classification. The estimated annual saving is ($.2825 − $.1360) $.1465 per volume equivalent stored in this mode. If the M.I.T. libraries stored all of the

[4]One must be careful in applying these factors since some libraries—M.I.T.'s included—count rebound pamphlets as "hardcover monographs."

present collection in compact form, the annual saving is estimated at ($.1465 × 510,000) $74,700. Again, given a doubling of the collection in eight years, the estimated annual saving resulting from compact storage would be $149,000.

If M.I.T. decided to store the entire collection in compact form, there would naturally be an initial cost of regrouping and rearranging. If M.I.T. did not store all the items this way, and this is certainly more likely, it would be necessary to weed the collection initially and periodically: to decide which books to store compactly, remove them, and change the catalog appropriately. It would also be necessary to provide a system to retrieve books from compact storage. To determine the annual savings from this method, a model was devised, taking into consideration the projected growth of the collection and alternative decision rules for weeding.

An Example of an Inexpensive Storage System

Comparison of Weeding Criteria: A Suboptimization

There are several criteria that are available for weeding book collections. We have considered the following:

1. Weeding by past circulation, i.e., by the number of times in a recent past period that the book was signed out of the library;

2. Weeding by publication date, i.e., remove all books published more than X years ago;

3. Weeding by acquisition date, i.e., remove all books acquired more than Y years ago;

4. Weeding by gross characteristics, i.e., remove all items exhibiting some particular characteristic, such as all books classified in the Dewey Decimal System.

We have assumed that a preliminary measure of the benefits foregone by storing some books inexpensively is the percentage of the total annual circulations attributable to books that are inconveniently located. A constant level of benefits thus implies a constant percentage of total circulations "stored" inexpensively. Note also that since more books are added to the libraries each year and since the use of books declines systematically with age (see Figure 5, based on the sample given in the next paragraph), the number of books stored inexpensively can rise each year without lowering aggregate benefits. The questions are then: For a given level of benefits, which criteria maximizes savings and what is the level of these savings?

In order to develop a picture of the popularity of the books that

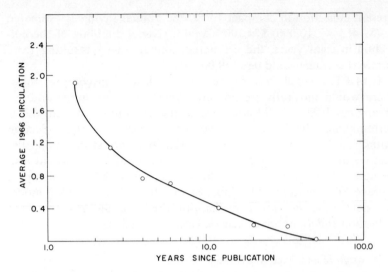

Figure 5.   Average 1966 circulation of a book as a function of x, the number of years since its publication.

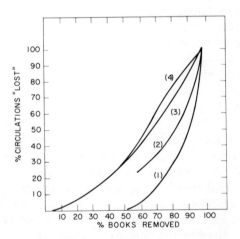

Figure 6.   Percent circulation "Lost" vs. percent books removed: (1) Foreknowledge; (2) Circulation criterion; (3) Publication date criterion; (4) Acquisition date criterion.

would be weeded by the various criteria considered in this report, we first selected a sample of 412 books from the second-floor stacks of the Dewey library (mainly social sciences).[5] From these volumes, we selected all those that were in the collection as of January 1963 ($N = 188$) and examined the results of hypothetical weeding programs had the collection been weeded in December 1963. With our data (Appendix 6), we were able to plot, for each of the weeding criterion, the percentage of books removed versus the percentage of 1964 to 1967[6] circulations "lost" (Figure 6). The "foreknowledge" curve shows what an optimal criterion would have produced.

As expected, past circulation is a good indicator of future use, while the acquisition and publication date criteria, both similar, are not as useful. The question, however, is whether the added cost of weeding by the circulation criterion cancels the additional storage savings due to the ability to store more books at a given level of benefits (i.e., circulations stored inconveniently).

Costs of Weeding

By Publication Date: The publication date can be determined by reading the catalog or examining the item. The latter method could be combined with actual weeding. The attractiveness of this method is that the catalog need not be changed to indicate which books have been removed. A sign of the type: "All books published before 1940 are now in storage" would be adequate for notifying users. We have examined two estimates of the cost of weeding by publication date, $.20 and $.40 per *volume equivalent.*

By Acquisition Date: This method is at best inferior to the publication date criterion. The cost of weeding is higher than with the publication date because the acquisition date is not on the catalog card and notifying users of a book's removal would necessitate a card catalog change. Furthermore, the publication date criterion allows the removal of at least as many books as with the acquisition date criterion for all levels of circulations lost. We consider this criterion dominated by the publication date criterion.

By Circulation Criterion: This method is very similar to Yale's method as reported by Ash. It required much individual attention to each book to count circulations on the withdrawal card. Furthermore, it is necessary to indicate on all the catalog cards associated

---

[5]See Philip M. Morse, *A Systems Approach to Library Effectiveness* (Cambridge, Mass.: The M.I.T. Press, 1968) for a more complete analysis of library circulation and models of library use.

[6]January 1964 through July 1967.

with the book that it has been stored. The Yale experiment found a cost per volume of $.61, but some weeding en masse had been done and fringe benefit and general administration costs were not included. We feel that $.80 to $1.00 per volume equivalent would be a more reasonable range of the cost of weeding by this criterion.

By Gross Characteristics of a Collection Subset: With this criterion, we are assuming we can characterize a given subset of books by its total circulation. We cannot graph a continuous plot for this criterion, for we either remove the entire set or not. The advantage here accrues when only a sign is needed to indicate that a particular subcollection has been removed to storage. Furthermore, as in the case with the Dewey Decimal System books in the Dewey library, these books are already housed as a separate collection. We estimate that $.03 per volume equivalent would be sufficient to remove such a collection.

One way to compare these costs is to treat weeding costs as capital expenditures and convert them into annual payments. The annual net saving at a particular level of benefits B for weeding criterion j is then given by the formula:

$$Nf_j(B) \{0.1465 - W_j[\text{c.r.f. } (i = 6\%; n = 50)]\} \qquad (6)$$

where N is the size of the collection in volume equivalents; $f_j(B)$ is the fraction of volumes equivalents removed by criterion j for the level of benefits B; W_j is the weeding cost per volume equivalent removed by criterion j; and c.r.f. is the 50-year, 6% capital recovery factor.

Table 9 gives the results of equation 6 for several levels of circulations "stored," i.e., benefits.

Table 9.   Annual Savings for Alternative Weeding Criteria

Percent Circulation "Lost" B	Percent Books Removed		Annual Net Savings for 510,000 Volume Equivalents			
	Circulation Criterion	Publication Date Criterion	Circulation Criterion $W_j =$		Publication Date Criterion $W_j =$	
	$f_j(B)$		$.80	$1.00	$.20	$.40
15%	47%	35%	$23,200	$19,900	$24,000	$21,700
20	54	42	26,500	22,800	28,700	26,000
25	62	47	30,500	26,200	32,100	29,200
50	83	69	40,800	35,100	47,200	42,800
75	94	86	46,300	39,800	59,000	53,500

We have concluded that for the collection characterized by our sample, the publication date criterion is probably more cost-effective, particularly at higher levels of circulations "stored." Given the greater decline in use of science books with age, the publication date criterion would probably prove superior for weeding science collections. The most useful criterion for humanities books was not determined, although it may *still* be more efficient to accept a loss in discriminating ability by using the publication date criterion rather than pay the added expense of determining past circulation patterns of books and changing the catalog for each book individually.

Dynamic Model Completed

Figure 7 combines projected growth data and specific weeding costs in order to compare "All Conventional Storage" with 25% of "Circulations Compactly Stored" over the next 15 to 20 years. In our accounting scheme, the cost of weeding is paid before savings are accrued. The length of this transition period depends on the cost of weeding and, of course, the interest rate (6%).

After such a transition period, the library would be storing those books which became X years old in the given year, and the savings would thus be a time-lagged function of the acquisitions rate. Although only a small percentage (10 to 20%) of the total amount that the libraries spend on storage can be saved each year by this storage policy, the accumulated savings would reach $368,000 in 15 years.[7]

Bringing Inexpensively Stored Books to the User: Retrieval Systems

If some books are placed in inexpensive storage outside the main collection, a system is needed to bring the user to those books or the books to the user. It is assumed that users would prefer the latter.

---

[7]Winston C. Lister in *Least Cost Decision Rules for the Selection of Library Material for Compact Storage* (Ph.D. Thesis, Purdue University, 1967), defines his total cost function as: Total Cost over H years = Building Costs + Maintenance and Operating Costs + Circulation Costs + Relocation Costs. Each of these costs is assumed to be either a constant per volume or a linear function of the number of volumes. Lister writes the total cost expression as a function of the "critical age"— the parameter defining which books should be removed to storage—and differentiates the total cost expression with respect to the "critical age" parameter to obtain the minimum cost conditions. In the formulation of the model, no attention is given to benefits or loss in benefits. In an unsuccessful attempt to remedy this, Lister introduces the concept of a shadow cost of the delay associated with books circulated from remote storage. The sensitivity of his "critical age" parameter to this shadow cost limits the usefulness of the derived minimum cost conditions.

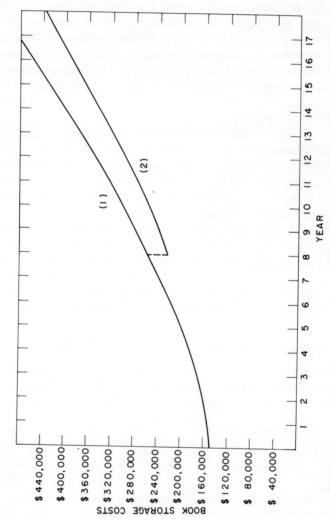

Figure 7.   Comparison of total cost for two storage alternatives: (1) Total M.I.T. storage cost, all conventional storage; (2) Total M.I.T. storage cost, 25% of circulations stored compactly, remainder stored conventionally.

A motorized system is necessary where library personnel cannot easily walk to retrieve books. For an independent motorized retrieval system at M.I.T., the cost was estimated to be about $17,000 per year, $15,000 of which would be for the additional personnel. The actual cost, however, would be lower if the cost of the system could be shared with some other function such as the proposed Wellesley-M.I.T. student transport service.

The cost of retrieval from decentralized, on-campus storage facilities (near current M.I.T. libraries) would be lower not only because personnel costs would be lower but also because the time per trip would be much smaller. The cost of such a decentralized system was estimated to be about $5,000 per year.

Consideration of retrieval systems adds weight to the conclusion that off-campus storage systems are not attractive. For example, the saving in compactly storing a book off campus as opposed to on campus is about $.015 per volume equivalent per year.[8] For 250,000 volume equivalents, about 50% of the present M.I.T. collection, the saving would be $3,750 annually, which would not be enough to cover the cost of the motorized retrieval system.

Microform Storage

The microform alternative is currently dominated by each of the other alternatives as a storage method because of the large cost of converting hardcover, print material to microfilm or microfiche. Current technology allows us to convert a page of print to microform for about $.02. A 400-page book would thus cost $8.00 to convert. Since we pay about $.28 a year to store the hardbound book, it would take almost 30 years just to pay for the original conversion without even considering interest charges, microform readers, or storage cabinets for the microforms. Without having to pay the cost of converting print to microform, a microform system is an inexpensive type of storage system. Its cost is very sensitive, however, to the number of microform readers the library installs. If the library provided one inexpensive reader, i.e., one costing $250, for every ten users (assuming 5-year amortization of readers), then the total annual storage cost for 200,000 volumes and 2,000 users would be approximately $10,000 or $.05 per volume. If the library installed alternatively 25% reader-printers, the cost would rise to

[8]This difference, it should be remembered, is due to differences in the price of land, on vs. off campus. For universities located in nonurban areas, this difference is probably smaller.

$32,000 annually or $.16 per volume. The first alternative is less than one-fifth of current per volume storage costs, while the second is about one-half of current costs. The attractiveness of microfiche storage thus depends on the amount and kind of reader equipment and the availability of the material in microform.

Storage of Books: Conclusion

We must conclude that altering the current storage system is not a very satisfactory way to save money.

The best alternative system, compact storage, saves only about 15% of current library expenditures on the storage of books, while storage expenditures themselves are only 6.4% of the annual budget. The saving, about 1% of annual library resources (less, if expensive retrieval systems are necessary), involves a major loss of benefits due to limitations on browsing and retrieval delay times of perhaps several hours.

3 Providing Study Space and Required Reading Material

Introduction

As the program budget indicates, the M.I.T. libraries spend 50%
more "storing" people in study spaces than they spend storing books
in stacks. A shortage in book storage space may be more observable, but the study space issue is more significant in terms of annual
costs.

The objective of the study-reserve system at M.I.T. is to provide
students with course-related materials and pleasant facilities to use
these materials. The present system includes (1) the reserve section
of the library; (2) library seats for studying and using reserve items;
(3) a source of textbooks, i.e., the Tech Coop (bookstore); (4) departmental reading and study rooms; and (5) dormitory room desks.
This report examines only the activities directly related to the library: the first two subsystems, which account for only about one-
third of the total amount spent by M.I.T. and its students on
required reading and studying.[1]

There are three basic methods of fulfilling the study-reserve function. First, the M.I.T. libraries can distribute (with or without
charge) course-related materials to students to be used primarily
in the dormitory rooms, libraries, and scattered study places. The
Coop presently sells books; in the future, the library could distribute or sell duplicated copies or microfiche cards of articles or entire
books.

[1]For example, on the assumption borne out by the Benefit Survey, that the average
M.I.T. student spends $100 annually on course-related books, the total outlay by
students on books would be $720,000, almost 50% more than the libraries' outlay for
reserve reading.

A second approach is to make the library the center of all required reading and to provide students with needed materials for limited amounts of time. This is the best method where the cost of an item is high and use of it is low. A third approach is to maintain the library as the central lending office but also to encourage students to duplicate and then remove those materials they want the most.

The Present Study-Reserve System

We estimate that the present library system costs about $517,000[2] annually, 38% for personnel, 38% for floor space (primarily study space), and 19% for books and duplicated articles.[3] There are several alternatives which would reduce the seating requirements of the library so that either current seating could be converted to stacks or the construction of new library facilities could be postponed despite an increase in the number of students (Appendix 7). The study-bedroom alternative has not been included as a separate alternative because improving study conditions in dormitory rooms without increasing user access to required reading—i.e., without changing the nature of the reserve system—will have little effect on library seating demands.

Alternative Study-Reserve Systems

Utilization of Adjacent Areas

The first alternative requires no funds but rather long-range planning. Future libraries could be built to be adjacent to or to encircle classrooms so that table-desk study places could be administered as part of the library during evening hours. To give present classrooms a "library" atmosphere, it might cost $5 a square foot, or about $.25 a square foot per year when allocated over 50 years, for more study space. Since such a plan requires classrooms to be near libraries, it would not greatly alter current seating requirements.

---

[2]This figure is less than the figure given in the program budget, because miscellaneous supplies have been excluded in order to cut down on the number of cost elements.

[3]The floor-space expense assumes that 75% of the current seating is used for study-reserve activities during peak hours. The program budget underestimates the cost per seat because the cost of furniture is added as an average cost across all activities to basic construction costs. However, study-space furniture has a relatively short life and is relatively more expensive. Furthermore, although the library reports a total of 1,788 seats, the number of "effective" or usable seats probably approaches 1,200. Given the current uncertainty about the use of seats in the library, it should be noted that seating costs are only rough estimates.

All Articles Xeroxed [4]

A second alternative is to sell or distribute articles or parts of books, as is now done with books through the Coop. The library would thus duplicate, for instance, all required articles and parts of books 60 pages or less and distribute them to all students enrolled in a course.[5]

It is our estimate that many of the users would use the printed articles outside the library. We calculated that the high volume of such a duplicating system would lower the cost per copy to $.0167 per page (with current technology). This amounts to an additional $87,000 annually. Since M.I.T. is now spending $196,300 on reserve seating, the demand for seating in the library would have to be reduced by about 45% in order to hold spending down to the present level. This is approximately the current percentage of items on reserve which would be distributed by this system, i.e., those of less than 60 pages. It is improbable, however, that all of these articles would be read outside the library. If seating is reduced by 25%, the system would cost about $38,000 more than the present system. Since the system is sensitive to seating demand and personnel requirements, a user behavior study and a further time survey of the reserve libraries are required to estimate costs more precisely.

Change Xerox Pricing

Another alternative would be to lower the price charged for Xeroxing rates to the local commercial level: $.05 for the first copy, $.03 for the second through tenth, and $.02 for additional copies. The added cost of this system depends on the relationship between the price of Xeroxing and the quantity demanded (i.e., the demand curve). Thus we examined a range of responses which would cost the library from $4,000 to $16,000 a year. To match current costs, this system would have to reduce current seating requirements by, at most, 5%. The range of seating demand savings

[4]For simplicity, the authors have used the term Xerox for all dry-copying processes.
[5]According to the Chief Legal Counsel to the Library of Congress, the new copyright law is designed to update and generally tighten the old one. Reproduction of copyrighted material by any means including computers, video electronics (i.e., CRT), Xerox, microfilm, etc., except for "fair use," without permission by or compensation to the author will be in violation of the law. For libraries this will mean that any large-scale systematic reproduction of parts of books, magazines, etc., such as the "Xerox All Articles" or "Microfiche" reserve systems, will involve copyright considerations. One estimate of the price that libraries may in the future have to pay publishers is as much as 10% of the cost of reproduction. This, it has been suggested, would be handled by an organization similar to BMI (Broadcast Music, Inc.).

was determined to vary from 0 to 10%, on the basis of estimates of the number of pages likely to be reproduced in this manner.

Lowering the Xerox price should have two other cost-cutting effects. First, circulation of certain types of material such as journals should decline, as more people reproduce journal articles; and second, the demand for seating to use journals and serials should decline. The latter effect, our Dewey library book survey indicates, may be more important than the reduction in seating demand associated with reserve material.

Microfiche Systems, Portable Readers

A fourth alternative which would reduce seating costs is a microfiche system, where all articles and parts of books 60 pages or less are put on microfiche and distributed to students. Each student is given a portable microfiche reader, primarily to be used in his dormitory room. Such a system would cost about $219,000 more than the present system and thus involves an additional cost that could not be recovered, regardless of any change in the demand for seats. It is quite possible, however, that technological advances will reduce the cost of microfiche readers. Yet, even if the reader prices fall by 50% and if the demand for seating in the library were halved, this alternative would still be dominated by the present system, i.e., for the same costs it would provide fewer benefits because of the complexities in using microfiche readers.

Another possibility would be for students to buy their own readers, but we believe that users would find the all-Xerox alternatives more attractive.

Microfiche, Readers in Dormitories and Libraries

Another proposed system, the dormitory-library microfiche system, would make it unnecessary for a student to travel to the library each time he wanted to do required reading. It would also allow him to maintain a permanent file of articles but would make students dependent on library-dormitory facilities for microfiche reading devices. Additional expense would be incurred from conversion and equipment purchase costs. We assumed that readers take up the same space as current seats in the library. Some of this cost is offset by decreased personnel costs resulting from decreased circulation and handling. The annual cost of this system is estimated to be $39,000 over that of the present system. If M.I.T. encouraged students to purchase their own portable readers, the demand for seating in the libraries would presumably shift downward, but under present conditions such a meaningful change in user behavior seems unlikely.

Providing Additional Copies of Required Reading and Extending Circulation Periods

Another method of reducing seating requirements is to provide more copies per article and to buy more copies of books in order to allow longer circulation periods (perhaps two days). It is estimated that providing three times the present ratio of ten students per copy would cost at least $56,400. This cost is based on the assumptions that books are not cataloged or processed, virtually all will be paperbacks, and that they are thrown away after they are taken off reserve. Even with such optimistic assumptions, seating demands would have to be reduced by 29% to maintain current expenditures.

Centralization

It has been suggested that the centralization of the reserve-study facilities would result in increased benefits and decreased costs. Benefits would increase because students would be able to do their work for any or all of their courses in one library; the chances of finding a specific item in one library would increase because of the concentration of copies of required readings; and the concentration of students would lead to greater social benefits. The decreased costs would result from economies of scale in the areas of personnel and seating.

As already indicated, personnel costs represent about 38% of current study-reserve expenditures. Yet almost all of these personnel costs, at least in the smaller reserve libraries, are for locating books, putting them on reserve, etc. rather than for circulation control or other costs which could be reduced by centralization.

A preliminary study of the cost of different types of seats indicated a wide inter-library difference in seating costs. For example, it was found that providing a lounge seat in the Lindgren library ($370) is almost twice as costly as the average Student Center lounge seat ($197). Part of this difference appears to be attributable to the availability of larger areas for seating in the Student Center and the resulting flexibility in planning seating arrangements. Another part of this difference is attributable to closer spacing and different combinations of facilities in the Student Center.

Table 10.   Comparative Seating Costs

Type	Number of Units in Group	Number of Seats in Unit	Number of Seats in Group	Area of Unit in Ft²	50-Year 6% per Unit Construction Costs per Year	Annual Maintenance Cost per Unit	Capital Cost of Furniture per Unit	15-Year 6% Furniture Cost per Unit per Year	Total Annual Cost per Unit	Total Annual Cost per Seat
Lounge setting:										
Student Center	15	1	15	28	$103.00*	$ 70.00	$236.00	$24.00	$197.00	$197.00
Dewey	6	1	6	56	135.00*	140.00	236.00	24.00	299.00	299.00
Lindgren	4	1	4	56	206.00*	140.00	236.00	24.00	370.00	370.00
Study tables:										
Student Center	12	4	48	84	309.00	210.00	312.00	32.00	551.00	138.00
Carrels:										
Student Center	5	2	10	76	280.00	190.00	270.00	28.00	498.00	249.00
Lindgren	6	2	12	63	232.00	158.00	160.00	16.00	406.00	203.00

*$58/ft² was the reported construction costs for the Student Center and the Green building (Lindgren library). However, a figure of $38/ft² was used for the Dewey library.

Table 10 shows comparative costs associated with seating accommodations for three recently built M.I.T. libraries.

Decentralization

The cost of decentralized, departmental reading-study libraries depends primarily on personnel requirements. Several examples of departmental reading-study libraries are suggested in Appendix 8.

A system of 10 departmental libraries to *supplement* the current study-reserve system would cost about $223,000 minus seating-savings more than the present "unsupplemented" system. Since these supplementary libraries would provide about 400 new seats, about 33% of the current (effective) seating, the expected seating savings (33%) would lower the additional annual cost to $158,000.

The cost of a system of 10 departmental libraries that would replace the divisional reserve collections would be about $114,000 more than the current system, $88,000 of which would be for additional personnel.

Divisional personnel would still be required to locate materials for departmental libraries when needed, and departmental libraries would be responsible for circulation control.

Study-Reserve Alternatives: Conclusion

In the preceding sections, we have analyzed alternative ways of providing course-related material and facilities to use this material. Because the costs of these alternatives are sensitive to the requirement for study space in the library, we have in Table 11 displayed the costs of these systems for a range of seating requirements. This range reflects a set of pessimistic, best guess, and optimistic predictions for the reduction in the demand for seating in the library.[6]

Appendix 9 breaks down the cost figures by personnel costs, study-space costs, special equipment costs, etc.

Suboptimizing Seating Accommodations in the Library

By "optimal seating accommodations," we mean a particular mix of seating accommodations within the study library that meets certain standards established by library administrators at minimum cost.

We believe that at least two types of standards, i.e., constraints, should be considered by library administrators: capacity constraints

[6]For conclusions with reference to the study-reserve function, see Chapter 6.

Table 11.   Summary of Reserve-Study Alternatives

	Annual Cost with Current Seating Demand	Annual Cost with Probable Seating Demand	Annual Cost with Optimistically Low Seating Demand
MICROFICHE SYSTEMS Each article and book section (60 pages or less) is placed on a microfiche card, duplicated, and distributed to students at the beginning of the semester or soon thereafter. Students maintain permanent files of assigned articles in the space of a shoebox. Readers are necessary to read the cards; dependence on reading devices is the price of guaranteed access to material. This system would supplement, not replace, books which are assigned.			
Portable Microfiche Readers Portable readers would be distributed to students for use primarily in their dorm rooms or home, thus guaranteeing access for all to a reader. A limited number of readers and reader-printers in the library would supplement portable readers.	$736,000	$696,800	$657,600
Library or Dormitory Microfiche Readers Readers would be distributed throughout campus, but students would not have guaranteed access to readers (and/or reader-printers). Students will always have the material but, depending on the level of the system (number of readers and reader-printers provided), would not always find a reader available.	556,000	*(10 Students/Reader)* 546,200	497,200
XEROX SYSTEMS These systems allow students to use the material at the time and place of their own choosing.			
All Article Xerox This system takes advantage of the lower per copy cost as volume is increased. Instead of providing an article per 10 students, the			

libraries would make enough copies for each student in the relevant course and would distribute these articles early in the semester.

Low-Cost Xerox

The library would lower the charge for Xeroxing to commercial rates, provide an operator, and encourage users to reproduce Library materials. Users could thus duplicate important materials at a low cost and would, to some degree, use the material outside of the library.

CONVENTIONAL SYSTEMS

These systems are based on the current technology of most libraries: books, limited Xeroxing, and microfiche.

Present System

We now have a reserve desk, collection, personnel, and reading area (or at least some seats used for required reading) in each of the divisional libraries. Supplementing these are independent libraries or reading rooms throughout campus directed by departments, research groups, or laboratories. The independent libraries, dormitory room desks, and the library study desks or halls, provide study spaces.

Departmental Libraries

Located near classrooms, these libraries would house 10 years of the 20 most used journals and a collection of 3,000 books. These libraries would also have about 20 table seats but provide no services beyond minimal cataloging. (In the future, they might be combined with graduate lounges and study areas.) Such libraries would either replace the current reserves system or would supplement it, thereby increasing the convenience and availability of required readings of recent vintage and, perhaps, lessening the seating requirements of the main libraries.

506,000	545,200	604,000
(*Elastic Demand: Total expenditure on Xeroxing increases*)		
501,400	519,000	521,000
(*Inelastic Demand: Total expenditure on Xeroxing decreases*)		
513,000	531,000	533,000
		517,000
		$740,000
		631,000
(*Supplemental*) $674,600		
(*Replacement*)		
$642,000		

Table 11 (Continued)

	Annual Cost with Current Seating Demand	Annual Cost with Probable Seating Demand	Annual Cost with Optimistically Low Seating Demand
Centralized Reserve Replacing the decentralized reserve systems with two main reserve-study centers (similar to the Student Center) would lessen the current convenience of the more localized reserve sections but would allow students to do all their work at one location.	433,500	433,500	368,800
Additional Copies Increasing the ratio of required readings to students from 1:10 to 1:3.3 for all books would increase the availability of materials, allow longer circulation periods, and reduce the number of seats required in the library because of present restricted circulations.	573,400 741,700	*(Low-Cost Assumptions)* 534,200 *(High-Cost Assumptions)* 702,500	495,000 663,300

ADDITIONAL PROPOSALS (AS YET NOT COSTED)

Adjacent Areas for Dual Purposes

This system takes advantage of different peak load times in different facilities. Both classrooms and cafeterias are not used as much at night when the strains on the library are greatest. By designing libraries to be adjacent to or to surround such areas, the tables could be used at night as part of the library at no extra cost.

Study Bedroom

This alternative is based on the notion that by making dormitory rooms more attractive for studying, it will encourage more people to return to them for study.

Subsidizing the Coop (Bookstore)

This alternative would provide money to allow the Coop to lower prices on required readings. It is expected that students would be encouraged to purchase their own books and thus use the library less.

(i.e., how many seats should be provided) and preference constraints (i.e., what is the relative "worth" of each type of seating accommodation). The reason for this is clear: There is an underlying conflict between providing, at a given budget level, the largest number of seats and providing the most attractive seats from the point of view of the user.

Capacity Constraints

Library administrators must decide on the percentage of students for which seating accommodations should be provided. Table 12 shows the current seating ratio for several large university libraries.

Table 12.   Seating Statistics for Larger University Libraries*
(Seats per 100 students)

	Current Library Seats	Current Seating Ratio	Ratio Expected 1970
Harvard	6,381	43.0	40.0–45.0
Yale	1,152	13.5	27.5
Princeton	2,946	62.0	73.0
M.I.T.	1,781	25.0	—
Columbia	4,208	25.0	37.0
California, Berkeley	4,591	17.0	24.0
Cornell	4,466	32.0	30.0
Stanford	4,000	36.0	36.0
Chicago	2,474	33.0	47.0
Michigan	5,783	20.5	—
Illinois	3,892	13.4	18.5
Pennsylvania	3,242	27.0	36.0

*From *College and Research Libraries* (November 1967), p. 412.

Preference Constraints

It has been tacitly assumed that students are not indifferent to the three types of seating accommodations and they will, in fact, prefer one type, if given a choice. Preference coefficients, let us assume, have been determined by asking students what type of accommodation—either lounge, table, or carrel—they use, or would most like to use. Since, we believe, preferences change as the term moves into its closing weeks, at least two determinations of the preference coefficients seem advisable.

The Optimal Mix by Linear Programming

Suppose, for this example, the libraries want to provide some seating for 25% of M.I.T. students (about 1,800 seats), and suppose also there is a desire to provide the "preferred" type of seating to the first 1,000 students. Then, let k_{ij} be the preference coefficient in the ith period for the jth type of seating. In this example, we are considering two periods and three types of accommodations (lounges, tables, and carrels).

Let L be the number of lounge units, T be the number of table units, and C be the number of carrel units. Then substituting seating costs from Table 10 into the total cost function, we obtain the linear programming problem

$$\min \$ = 197\,L + 551\,T + 498\,C$$

subject to

$$L + 4T + 2C \geq 1{,}800 \quad \text{(capacity constraint)}$$

$$k_{11}L + k_{12}T + k_{13}C \geq 1{,}000$$
$$\qquad\qquad\qquad\qquad\qquad\qquad \text{(preference constraints)}$$
$$k_{21}L + k_{22}T + k_{23}C \geq 1{,}000$$

If the k_{ij} are known, the problem can be solved for the optimal mix L, T, and C, and the total cost. Because of the absence of data to establish such constraints, we offer this analysis as an example of a suboptimization within a general systems analysis.

4 Fulfilling Research Requirements

Introduction

The Program Budget of the M.I.T. libraries has indicated not only the large cost of providing study spaces but also the large (and growing) costs of building the collection.

The discussion that follows describes some of the real alternatives that relate to the problems of building the collection and fulfilling research needs. Table 13 lists systems relating to alternative cataloging schemes, alternative ordering schemes, enlarged "extra-M.I.T." retrieval systems, improved access to other collections, and improved selection.

Table 13.   Systems Relating to Research Needs

A. Alternative Cataloging Schemes
    1. Current system
    2. Limited cataloging
    3. Temporary cataloging
    4. Augmented catalog
    5. Additional catalogs
    6. Project MARC cataloging
B. Alternative Ordering Schemes
    1. Delayed ordering
    2. Fast ordering
    3. Xeroxing from interlibrary loan
C. "Extra-M.I.T." Retrieval System
    1. Direct messenger service
    2. Internal speedup of interlibrary service
    3. Library of Congress messenger service
D. Access to Other Collections
    1. User transportation to nearby collections
    2. User transportation to distant collections
    3. Catalogs of other collections on M.I.T. campus
E. Improved Selection and Acquisition
    1. "Better selection"—fewer books
    2. Common acquisitions policy with sister school

Alternative Cataloging Schemes

The largest processing cost is for cataloging. We have examined the expenses involved in cataloging items to determine where savings are possible. Table 14 breaks down cataloging expenses by activity and separates the professional and nonprofessional contributions. The major item is classifying of items by professional librarians, which costs the library (50% × $196,500) $98,250 annually. It would probably be worthwhile to determine the effects of lowering this cost by "limited" cataloging. This might take the form of reducing the time spent by professional catalogers, limiting the number of subject references for a given book, or perhaps not subject cataloging "difficult" cases at all. Another area of possible savings is in the proofreading and checking of catalog cards which currently costs the library about $46,000 annually. It would be necessary, however, to know the effect of errors and other shortcomings in the catalog on the level of benefits.

Table 14.   Cataloging Costs by Activity and Personnel

Activity	Time Spent by Professional Librarians	Time Spent by Nonprofessional Librarians
Classifying	50%	4%
Proofreading, checking	17	10
Typing	17	28
Searching for LC Card	8	7
Placing Cards in Catalog	6	25
LC Cataloging	1	16
Total Moneys (with fringe benefits, library administration, general administration costs included)	$196,500	$134,000

Alternatively, what benefits would accrue to a more elaborate cataloging scheme such as Project INTREX's "Augmented Catalog?" A complete assessment can probably only be made when Project INTREX's Augmented Catalog at M.I.T. is operational.[1]

Cost figures seem to indicate that the money saved in waiting for the Library of Congress (LC) cards is substantial. The library currently reports that about 30% of the books cataloged are "non-LC," i.e., books for which LC cards are not on hand. Up to $55,000 per year could be saved if original cataloging were eliminated and these

[1]See Carl F. J. Overhage and R. Joyce Harman (eds.), *INTREX: The Report of a Planning Conference on Information Transfer Experiments* (Cambridge, Mass.: The M.I.T. Press, 1965) for a discussion of future technology and libraries.

books were LC cataloged whenever the cards arrived. However, delaying cataloging will inescapably lead to a decrease in benefits. Notifying the requester or potential user of a book's arrival may help to overcome some of the loss. Perhaps temporary "in-house" cataloging of non-LC books may prove valuable.

In order to evaluate this last possibility, information on the number of non-LC books cataloged last year, the distribution of delays, and the average number of potential uses should be obtained.

It is true, however, that the Library of Congress is cataloging a higher percentage of all monographs (see Figure 8) each year under

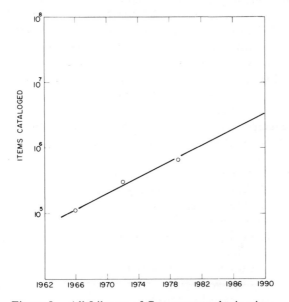

Figure 8.   All Library of Congress cataloging including Title II C through 1990.

Title IIC, and the average cataloging cost per book should continue to decline. In 1965, 68% of American imprints were cataloged before publication. By 1970, the Library of Congress expects this to climb to 75%. Thus not only is the Library of Congress cataloging a higher percentage of books each year under Title IIC, but they are also improving the speed of service.

An Analysis of Temporary Cataloging

Each year M.I.T. does original cataloging for about 10,000 monographs at a cost of about $150,000. Suppose that temporary cataloging could be done at one-third the cost of original cataloging.[2] This is close to the cost of "recataloging" and is, no doubt, too low an estimate. This was deliberately done to weight the argument in favor of "temporary cataloging." Suppose also that it is M.I.T. policy to do the original cataloging on imprints for which the expected delay in receiving the LC cards is greater than six months. Since these are usually foreign language publications, library personnel have little difficulty in identifying this subset.

If it is assumed that 10% of the 10,000 non-LC books fall into this subset, then the cost of cataloging them is (1000 × $15) $15,000. The remaining 90% of non-LC books are "temporarily" cataloged at first at a cost of (9000 × $5) $45,000, and then LC cataloged, when the LC cards arrive, at a cost of (9000 × $9.45) $85,000. If these temporarily cataloged books have been put into the stacks there would be an additional cost of at least $.50 per book to track down and retrieve them to be LC cataloged. This would entail an additional cost of (9000 × $.50) $4,500.

At this point the *a fortiori* argument is made that the savings from the temporary cataloging scheme described above are so small that the decrease in benefits cannot be justified.

A.	Current Original Cataloging Cost:	$150,000/yr
B.	Cost of Temporary Cataloging Scheme:	
	1. Temporary cataloging of 90% non-LC books	45,000/yr
	2. Retrieving these books to be LC cataloged	4,500/yr
	3. LC cataloging of these books	85,000/yr
	4. Original cataloging for remaining 10% of non-LC books	15,000/yr
		$149,500/yr

Net savings: $500/yr

Project MARC

Another interesting alternative will soon be possible when the Library of Congress's Project MARC begins selling machine-readable catalog information on magnetic tape for all English language books plus some German and French monographs. Presently,

[2]Temporary cataloging means that books arriving at the library without LC cards are briefly cataloged to provide a minimum of information. The temporary card is later replaced by the LC permanent and more complete card. Original cataloging is done more completely, for the cards are not later replaced by LC cards.

these tapes can only be used to duplicate the LC cards but eventually could become the input data to a computerized on-line catalog.

The cost to subscribers of this weekly service has been set at $600 per year.

Alternative Ordering Schemes

Since handling, not cataloging, is the main processing cost of journals and serials, $20 per journal could be saved if the journals were purchased on commercially produced microfilm.

This saving would be accompanied by a loss in benefits because microfilm can only be purchased at the end of the year. Alternatively, more journals than the M.I.T. library currently receives could be purchased at the current budget level if the microfilm version were specified.

This is particularly significant since the number of journals (and average price) has been increasing (see Appendix 10). Thus, with current policies, in order to maintain the same percentage of coverage, the library will by 1976 have to allocate twice as much money as now for serials and journals. This will not be a burden, however, so long as materials appropriations grow at this rate too. Figure 9 shows the materials appropriations projected through 1976.[3]

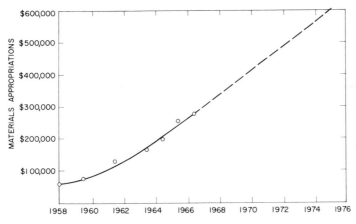

Figure 9.   M.I.T. materials appropriations projected through 1974.

[3] These figures include the Dewey, Engineering, Humanities, Rotch, and Science libraries.

Extra-M.I.T. Retrieval Systems

There are several proposals which would decrease the time between a request for an item not in the M.I.T. libraries and its delivery.

The first alternative, a direct messenger service run by M.I.T. for M.I.T. users, would retrieve requested books as soon as the lending library in the Boston area indicated that it had located the book. It would also bring request slips directly and immediately to local schools. Such a fast service would cost from $5,000 to $12,000 annually, depending on the volume of such loans, the number of hours the system would be in operation, and the number and location of participating libraries. This system would thus limit waiting time to the reaction time of the lending library.

The delays in obtaining books on interlibrary loan may be caused by intralibrary rather than interlibrary procedures. The cost of reducing such delays would vary with each participating library and would have to be based on cooperative agreements.

In determining the level of expenditures for interlibrary loan, it is necessary to determine not only the cost of purchasing and processing a book but also the use of the book as a function of time. With an elaborate loan system, a book ordered through interlibrary loan might incur a cost of $20 a request. In terms of present value, the cost of fulfilling that request 5 years in the future is about $15, and for 10 years in the future about $11. Thus, the comparison must be in terms of the present cost of purchasing and processing, and the present value of the costs of borrowing the book to meet future requests.

For those books which are difficult to locate in the Boston metropolitan area, a more expensive but longer range retrieval system is possible. A messenger could be sent to the Library of Congress in Washington, D.C., for under $100 per trip including salary. Making the trip twice a week, 40 weeks per year, the cost of such a system would be $8,000 a year. Borrowing two books a week this way would bring the cost to $100 a book; twenty books weekly would average out to $10 a book—the cost of interlibrary loan! It would be necessary to determine the percentage of requested books which the local and LC systems could handle.

Access to Other Collections

The first alternative for increasing access to other libraries would be to provide a transportation system (where a public system is limited or nonexistent) for users to travel to other collections. This alternative appears attractive where external economies exist, e.g., where the cost of transportation is shared by more than one system. Given the pressures on libraries to provide seats when such a system would be most desirable, its use appears to be limited.

Occasionally a user requires specialized items in areas not covered in local libraries. The size of the budget for travel (to the West Coast, Paris, South America) to distant collections is, of course, a function of the frequency of such needs.

A microstrip catalog of M.I.T.'s entire union catalog could fit, with a microstrip reader, on a desk top. The initial cost of converting the catalog (say one million volumes) would be about $50,000. The cost of duplicating such a catalog would be about $2,500 per copy. Appendix 11 lists the costs of four arrangements with other libraries where the costs per library (assuming an equal sharing of costs) range from $38,785 to $257,250 initially. Added to the initial cost of duplication is the cost of reduplicating or maintaining an additional catalog for items acquired after the initial duplication. This would cost at least $25,000 annually. Catalog duplication is thus a very expensive alternative.

On-line computerized catalogs will be ideal for this purpose once made operational for such a searching procedure. Closed-circuit television connecting users to other libraries has not worked in the past but, given proper investments, might be a solution. A telephone "hot line," run by special librarians at the remote library, might encourage people to find out what is available in other libraries. A librarian or less skilled person at each school could handle about 5,000 requests annually at a cost of under $10,000. Given the high costs of other systems, this may be the most interesting alternative.

Improved Selection and Acquisition

It is an observable fact that the number of books, pamphlets, and periodicals has been increasing for many years (see Appendix 12). Furthermore, book prices and serial prices have also been rising, and at a rate greater than the overall price index (see Figure 10). Table 15 combines publisher's output data with price data to show that, with current selection policies, resources programmed for acquisitions will have to double every six to eight years. Even then it is possible that the M.I.T. libraries may be unable to acquire a significant portion of "desirable" material. It should also be noted that it will be relatively more costly to maintain an up-to-date science and technology collection than a social science collection.

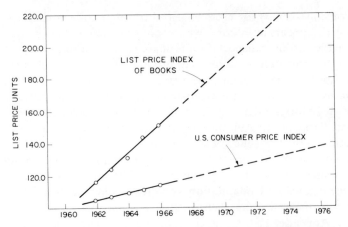

Figure 10. List price index of books (hardcover, trade-technical) projected through 1976 (1957–1959 = 100.0).

Table 15.   Number of New Editions and Titles Published from 1962 and Projected through 1976

New Editions and Titles

	1962	1966	1972	1976
A. Nonfiction, hardbound only	16,600 @$ 6.00 =$ 99,600	25,300 @$ 8.00 =$202,400	38,600 @$ 10.25 =$395,650	47,300 @$ 12.60 =$595,980
B. Nonfiction, paperbound	4,400 @$ 2.10 =$ 9,240	8,100 @$ 2.80 =$ 22,680	11,400 @$ 4.20 =$ 47,880	15,100 @$ 5.00 =$ 75,500
C. All nonfiction, hard and paper	21,000	33,400	50,000	62,400
D. Total Cost (A + B)	$108,840	$225,080	$443,530	$671,480

New Editions and Titles by Category

	1962	1966	1972	1976
A. Science and technology	3,200 @$ 9.80 =$ 31,360	5,600 @$ 12.50 =$ 70,000	9,200 @$ 16.70 =$153,640	12,000 @$ 19.60 =$235,200
B. Sociology, economics, business, and history	4,050 @$ 7.70 =$ 31,185	7,000 @$ 9.00 =$ 63,000	11,800 @$ 10.90 =$128,620	14,800 @$ 12.10 =$179,080

To demonstrate the magnitude of possible savings from better selection, the percentage of books would have to be known that have been in the collection for some long period, say 15 years, but have had no more than one or possibly two "significant uses" in that period. Each of these books represents an investment of about $25 (selection, purchase price, cataloging, storage, etc.). Were a book not acquired, this amount, minus both the cost of better selection and a charge for providing the book by some alternative fast means (such as an improved interlibrary loan), could be saved. If it is assumed that the level of benefits is measured by the number of significant uses, then the loss in benefits would be extremely small.

In order to evaluate different selection policies, information would have to be known about yearly expected circulations (or better, yearly circulation probability density functions) for books in different subject areas, chosen according to selection plans at different budget levels.[4]

Comparing Alternative Selection Plans

A First Attempt at Modeling Selection Principles

The optimization principle here is that for a given level of benefits, the library seeks to minimize the total cost of selecting, ordering, purchasing, cataloging, and storing its new acquisitions for, say, 15 years. All of these costs, except selection, can be aggregated into a single average cost (a membership fee) per new acquisition.

To state this mathematically, let m be the membership fee (say $25), N the number of new acquisitions, S the aggregate selection costs, $C(N, S)$ the number of significant uses of new acquisitions, i.e., benefits. Here $C(N, S)$ is a continuous and twice-differentiable function of its arguments.

Then the library seeks to minimize $mN + S$ subject to $C_0 = C(N, S)$. The optimization condition is

$$m = \frac{\partial C / \partial N}{\partial C / \partial S}$$

This model requires strict knowledge of the marginal contribution to benefits of a new acquisition and the marginal contribution to benefits of a dollar spent on selection. Operationally, the library should be able to increase its S-budget (selection) by X dollars and decrease its mN-budget (purchasing-processing) by $Y \geq X$ dollars, in order to secure the same number C_0 of significant uses.

[4] See Philip M. Morse, *A Systems Approach to Library Effectiveness* (Cambridge, Mass.: The M.I.T. Press, 1968) for a good discussion of selection policy models.

The key assumption in this model is that *ceteris paribus*[5] the number of significant uses of new acquisitions is a function only of the selection budget and the number of new acquisitions. So long as alternative means (such as interlibrary loan) of creating "significant uses" account for only a small percentage of the total number of significant uses,[6] this assumption is defensible.

Another Model

Table 16 shows how alternative combinations of inputs— money for books and money for selection—might relate to hypothetical levels of outputs—number of new acquisitions and number of significant uses in 15 years. This model represents an improvement over the one in the previous section since there is now a primary benefit, which is the number of significant uses, and a secondary benefit, the number of books. In cost-benefit terms, if the number of books is seen as an independent benefit measure and the budget is fixed at $305,000, alternative E would *dominate* alternative F, because it provides more benefits (more books and equal number of significant uses) at the same cost. If the number of books is not considered an independent measure of benefits, the library decision-makers must decide whether to spend the marginal $25,000 on book purchasing, as in alternative E, or in selection, as in alternative F. When displayed in this way, trade-offs between spending money on selection and spending money on book purchasing become evident.

Any estimates of the net benefits would also have to include the number of unsuccessful attempts to locate a book in the library and the disutility of not having those books for each one of the alternatives.

Table 16.   Hypothetical Output Levels Associated with Varying Selection Inputs

	Inputs			Outputs	
Alternative	Money for Books, $25 N_0	Money for Selection	Total	Number of New Acquisitions, N_0	Number of Significant Uses in 15 Yr from N_0 Books
A	$250,000	$10,000	$260,000	10,000	90,000
B	$150,000	$25,000	$175,000	6,000	72,000
C	$200,000	$20,000	$220,000	8,000	84,000
D	$250,000	$ 5,000	$255,000	10,000	86,000
E	$300,000	$ 5,000	$305,000	12,000	92,000
F	$275,000	$30,000	$305,000	11,000	92,000

[5] I.e., for a given number of users, for a particular mode of storage, etc.
[6] Presently, interlibrary loan accounts for about 0.5% of total circulation.

Common Acquisition with Wellesley

Another important alternative is for M.I.T. to seek some form of common acquisition policy with another nearby research library. Because of the new degree of cooperation, one school suggests itself immediately—Wellesley. Figure 11 projects the research acquisition rate for both M.I.T. and Wellesley, the latter being measured from the M.I.T. curve. If the acquisition rates were fully additive, which of course they are not, the total rate would about cover the projected publisher's output of nonfiction through 1976 (Appendix 12). Naturally, a common acquisitions policy must be accompanied by commonality of user services and privileges. In addition, some user transportation scheme and an improved interlibrary loan system would become desirable.

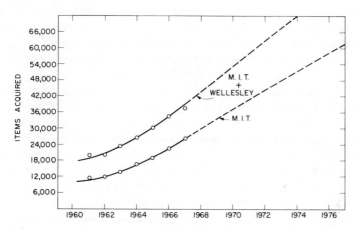

Figure 11.   M.I.T. and Wellesley annual acquisitions projected through 1976.

5 Benefit Evaluation

Desirable Characteristics of Benefit Measures

Much of the analysis that has been presented so far has relied primarily upon impressionistic judgments of the benefits associated with a given system and of comparisons among systems serving different objectives. The goal of this chapter is to present a more quantitative measure of library effectiveness. Before presenting this technique and its limitations, however, some problems associated with traditional measures ought to be discussed.

In the past, quantitative measures of library performance have generally been based on library *efficiency* rather than library *effectiveness*.[1] The reason for this is clear: It is a matter of relative ease to measure the number of times the system fails in N trials, but it is quite difficult to measure the number of successes in an undefined population, particularly since it is not exactly clear what constitutes a success. Any sample taken of people entering the library systematically excludes those who have "given up altogether." How can the library's role in fostering inadvertent discovery (browsing, etc.) be gauged? How can the value (utility) of a "success" be measured, and if it can, what part of that value is attributable to the library? Clearly if only a few users among numerous potential users are satisfied, the library is not effective, although it may be efficiently finding books for those users.[2] We believe that one of the problems in measuring the benefits of the library, or of its subsystems, is the lack of definite quantifiable, tangible objectives to be attained. In the first attempt to model selection principles (Chapter 4), this quality was present: to attain C_0 significant uses. This production

---

[1] For example, G. C. Bush, H. P. Galliher, and P. M. Morse, "Attendance and Use of the Science Library at M.I.T.," *American Documentation*, Vol. VII, No. 2, pp. 87–109.

[2] See David Novick, *Program Budgeting* (Cambridge, Mass.: Harvard University Press, 1965), pp. 48–51, for a discussion of efficiency and effectiveness.

function model was quickly discarded in favor of a more complex model. A measure of library effectiveness must take serendipity, use encouragement, and other intangibles into account.

A second problem in measuring library benefits is that different subgroups may prefer different systems. Thus a library which has a large and efficient reference staff is not necessarily an effective library for undergraduates seeking course-required books on closed reserve. Undergraduates might attach higher benefits to having more reserve books available rather than more librarians. Thus a measure of a library's effectiveness cannot be separated from the (potential) users of the library.

This leads to another consideration in evaluating alternative allocations of library resources, the social welfare implications. The allocation of a fixed budget represents a set of decisions about which functions should be fulfilled, and thus which objectives should be met and which users should be satisfied at the relative expense of other objectives and users. For example, it is estimated that the M.I.T. community spends $1,350,000 annually to provide required reading to students, about 40% of this from library funds (or 25% of the library budget), 10% from dormitory expenditures, and 50% from students.[3] In comparison, about 75% of the library's funds is allocated for the research objective. Can any benefit measure weigh the benefits of meeting the research objective with those of meeting the objective of providing course material? We submit that although the decision at this point, when comparing objectives measured along different dimensions, is political (i.e., choosing which set of values shall prevail), a preferred benefit measure should make explicit the trade-offs that can be made. Thus the basic points are: (1) if possible, community rather than institutional costs and benefits should be considered; and (2) the budget represents a political decision with social welfare implications because different groups benefit from different allocations.[4]

A fourth difficulty is relating streams of costs and benefits. How can one compare having a seat available today with having to wait

---

[3] The results of a question on the benefit survey (to be discussed later) indicate that the average student spends $110 and faculty members $130 annually on books.

[4] For a discussion of these issues in economic and political theory, see: Willmoore Kendall and George W. Carey, "The 'Intensity' Problem and Democratic Theory," *American Political Science Review*, Vol. LXII (March 1968), pp. 5–24; Anthony Downs, *An Economic Theory of Democracy* (New York: Harper & Row Publishers, 1957); and Kenneth J. Arrow, *Social Choice and Individual Values* (New York: John Wiley & Sons, Inc., 1951).

for the same seat for five minutes next year? Do individuals have a personal discount rate not congruent with annual rates of return but related to psychological needs for instant or delayed gratification? A more quantitative discussion of this question arose in the earlier analysis of storage alternatives.

These examples of difficulties associated with measuring library benefits are meant to be suggestive, not exhaustive. Survey research allows one to bypass several of these problems.

Measuring Benefits by Survey Research Procedures

One method of measuring incommensurables and trade-offs among systems serving different objectives is the use of judges to rank alternative systems. Such judges are asked to compare all possible pairs of systems at different budget levels. If we want to compare n alternatives at the same budget level, then $C_2^n = n!/[(n - 2)! \, 2!]$ comparisons must be made in order to obtain an overall ranking of alternatives. Scherer suggests that the choices of individual respondents can be aggregated by means of scaling factors into a group consensus ranking.[5] For any alternative A, the scaling factor is defined as the number of times A was chosen over other programs divided by the total number of choices involving A.

If there is "significant evidence of intransitivity in the individual respondent's paired comparisons" or if there is "little agreement among the various respondents on their ranking of the different alternatives," then this procedure would suffer from a lack of validity.[6] For this reason, such a method was not adequate for this analysis, because a universal ranking of alternative systems (i.e., in terms of social welfare to M.I.T. as a unit) could not be assumed. The rankings of individuals or subgroups were desired so that alternatives could be compared as to their differing desirability rather than differentially perceived value across individuals. Furthermore, since it was desirable to attain evaluations from nonlibrary users and sufficient subgroup members to permit cross tabulations, and since with say, 20 systems, 190 comparisons would be required of each individual, a more limited survey method was developed.

[5] Frederic M. Scherer, "Government Research and Development Programs" in Robert Dorfman (ed.), *Measuring Benefits of Government Investments* (Washington, D.C.: The Brookings Institution, 1965).

[6] *Ibid.*, p. 32.

Unlike past user surveys, this evaluation provided respondents with information as to the costs of each system. This allowed the respondent to alter the current budgetary allocation scheme by trading systems. The survey did not ask for a simple like-dislike answer, and it allowed respondents to evaluate future systems. Essentially, the survey asked respondents to make the trade-offs and comparisons done by library decision-makers, but in terms of what they desired, not what they thought others sought. It skirts the problem noted earlier by forcing individuals to compare alternatives implicitly, i.e., to make individual value judgments, so that the analyst may make explicit comparisons.

Included in the questionnaire were:

1. A cover letter sent by the Director of Libraries asking for the respondent's cooperation and briefly describing the study;

2. A list of 20 alternatives derived from the cost analysis with brief descriptions of the benefit gains or losses entailed by each system and its annual cost;

3. An instruction sheet; and

4. An answer sheet and traditional questions about library use, department, etc.

The instructions essentially asked respondents to weigh the costs and benefits of 20 library systems and choose those they preferred at three different budget levels (The complete questionnaire is reproduced as Figure 12).

Problems and Limitations of Surveying Benefits

Of the 700 surveys mailed to faculty members and students, 283 or 40% were returned. This response rate, although not low for mail surveys, does limit generalizing from the returned questionnaires to the entire M.I.T. population. The low rate was probably a result of the time it was sent out, approximately two weeks before exam week. Nonresponders may have been those who were least interested in changing or improving the libraries or, alternatively, those who were most upset about the library facilities and services.[7] The time of the year did not permit a follow-up study to test these hypotheses,

---

[7]Although a precise determination of this question is impossible, the response rates for faculty and students were identical, i.e., there was no differential response rate by M.I.T. status.

May 7, 1968

Dear Member of the M.I.T. Community:

You have been selected by random sampling to assist the M.I.T. Libraries by providing data to help in planning library operations for the period extending through 1980. Students, faculty members, and researchers in the M.I.T. community are being asked to aid in a long-range study by filling out the enclosed questionnaire concerning new library buildings, acquisition policies, and technological innovations.

We would appreciate your returning this questionnaire within one week by Institute mail. An addressed envelope has been enclosed for your convenience.

Completion of this survey will take you about 15 minutes. Information about the costs of alternatives has been provided so that you may better judge the allocation of library resources. We hope that you will take advantage of this opportunity to play a significant role in the decision-making process.

Thank you for your cooperation.

Sincerely,

William N. Locke
Director of Libraries

WNL/jry
Enclosures

Instructions

Attached are descriptions of 20 alternative systems designed to improve library service and/or to save money. For each of the three *supplemental* library budgets indicated below, you are asked to weigh the costs and benefits of these alternative systems and then to select those systems you wish to "buy."

1. Given a supplemental budget of $200,000.
2. Given a supplemental budget of $100,000.
3. Given no new funds i.e., $0. If you wish to purchase new systems you must save money on some other systems.

Negative costs are of course *savings*. Thus a system costing "$ – 100,000" saves the library $100,000 and gives you an additional $100,000 to spend on other library services.

You should attempt to spend all of the money given to you, but do not worry if you are less than $15,000 off. Please indicate on the ANSWER SHEET the systems you want by checking the boxes next to the numbers corresponding to those systems. You should find it convenient to use the blank columns to compute the total cost of the systems you prefer. There is in addition a BACKGROUND DATA SHEET. Please complete this, too.

Figure 12.   Benefit survey.

Alternative	Benefit Considerations	Annual Additional Cost to Present Library Budget
1. 50% of the library's holdings of books which account for about 25% of total library circulations for the year, would be removed to an on-campus storage facility. There, these books would be stored as they are presently arranged (i.e., according to conventional Library of Congress classification) but access to the stacks would be restricted. Librarians would retrieve requested books on demand.	1. Browsing possible only under special circumstances, such as for theses, special projects, etc. Users would also encounter an average delay of 1/2 hour to retrieve stored books.	1. $-10,000
2. Again, 50% of the library's holdings of books which account for about 25% of total library circulations for the year, would be removed to an on-campus storage facility. There, these books would be stored *compactly* (i.e., shelved chronologically and by size). Access to the stacks would be closed, and librarians would retrieve requested books on demand. (Note: 1 and 2 cannot *both* be selected.)	2. Browsing impossible since books are not stored by subject classification. Users would also encounter an average delay of 1/2 hour to retrieve stored books.	2. $-25,000
3. *Expand* seating (all types) in libraries by *10%*. (Note: From systems 3 through 6, only one may be selected.)	3. Users would be able to find "choice" seating accommodations more easily.	3. $+25,000
4. *Expand* seating (all types) in libraries by *20%*.	4. Users would be able to find "choice" seating accommodations more easily.	4. $+50,000
5. *Cut* seating (all types) in libraries by *10%*.	5. Users would find it more difficult to obtain a seat in the library.	5. $-25,000
6. *Cut* seating (all types) in libraries by *20%*.	6. Users would find it more difficult to obtain a seat in the library.	6. $-50,000
7. The decentralized reserve collections would be replaced by two main reserve-study centers (one already in the Student Center, and another similar facility located near the Sloan-Hermann complex). Overnight circulation would be permitted from this latter facility. Areas now in the libraries devoted to study-reserve would be converted into stacks.	7. Replacing the decentralized reserve systems with two main study-reserve centers would lessen the current convenience of the more localized reserve collections, but would allow students to do all their work at one location.	7. $-75,000
8. The library would lower the charge for Xeroxing to local commercial rates, provide an operator, and encourage users to reproduce library material.	8. Users could duplicate important material at low cost and would be able to use the material outside the library.	8. $+10,000

Figure 12 (Continued)

Alternative	Benefit Considerations	Annual Additional Cost to Present Library Budget
9. Ten supplemental *departmental* libraries located near class-rooms would be built to house 10 years of the 20 most used journals and a collection of 3,000 books, including some required and recommended reading. These libraries would also have about 15 seats, but would provide no services beyond minimal cataloging. These might be contiguous to graduate lounges and study areas.	9. Such departmental libraries would provide more conveniently located working collections, and increase the availability of required and recommended reading.	9. $+160,000
10. Instead of providing a reserve article per 10 students, the libraries would make enough complete Xerox copies of all articles 60 pages or less for *each* student in the relevant course and would distribute these articles.	10. Students could have a complete file of required articles for future use, and could read and study them at any time, in or out of the library.	10. $+80,000
11. *Increase* annual acquisitions by *10%*. (Note: From systems 11 through 14, only one may be selected.)	11. Libraries could buy more new books as well as older books to "round out" the M.I.T. collection.	11. $+80,000
12. *Increase* annual acquisitions by *20%*.	12. Libraries could buy more new books as well as older books to "round out" the M.I.T. collection.	12. $+160,000
13. *Decrease* annual acquisitions by *10%*.	13. Libraries could buy fewer books.	13. $-80,000
14. *Decrease* annual acquisitions by *20%*.	14. Libraries could buy fewer books.	14. $-160,000
15. The amount of time spent by professional catalogers on each book would be limited to a shorter period. The proof-reading and checking of catalog cards would also be curtailed.	15. The number of subject references for a given book would be limited. There would also be minor errors and other shortcomings in the catalog.	15. $-75,000
16. The library would cut its reference staff by *10%*.	16. Bibliographic services and information aids would suffer.	16. $-25,000
17. The library would add to its reference staff by *10%*.	17. Bibliographic services and information aids would be improved.	17. $+25,000
18. The library would implement a direct telephone line to, say, Wellesley, staffed by additional professional librarians on station at Wellesley. In addition, interlibrary loan would be im-	18. Users would be able to find out about books at another university library and would be able to obtain books within hours.	18. $+30,000

Figure 12 (Continued)

proved by increasing internal operating efficiency and direct messenger pickup.

19. The library would operate a long-range messenger service to the Library of Congress in Washington.

20. The library would purchase paperbacks of about 1/2 of books on reserve. This would treble the book:student ratio from 1:10 to 3:10. Circulation periods for these books would be lengthened to two days.

19. Users would be able to obtain books from the Library of Congress if they could not be obtained from a nearby collection.

20. Users would find required reading more readily available and would be able to take out these books for longer periods.

19. $ + 10,000

20. $ + 50,000

Figure 12   (Continued)

ANSWER SHEET

Alternative	Cost	$200,000 Budget	$100,000 Budget	$0 Budget
1. Conventional Storage Facility	$ −10,000	1. ☐	1. ☐	1. ☐
2. Compact Storage Facility	$ −25,000	2. ☐	2. ☐	2. ☐
3. Expand Seating 10%	$ +25,000	3. ☐	3. ☐	3. ☐
4. Expand Seating 20%	$ +50,000	4. ☐	4. ☐	4. ☐
5. Cut Seating 10%	$ −25,000	5. ☐	5. ☐	5. ☐
6. Cut Seating 20%	$ −50,000	6. ☐	6. ☐	6. ☐
7. Two Centralized Study-Reserve Libraries	$ −75,000	7. ☐	7. ☐	7. ☐
8. Lower Xerox Rates	$ +10,000	8. ☐	8. ☐	8. ☐
9. Ten Departmental Libraries	$ +160,000	9. ☐	9. ☐	9. ☐
10. All-Xerox Reserve	$ +80,000	10. ☐	10. ☐	10. ☐
11. Increase Annual Acquisitions by 10%	$ +80,000	11. ☐	11. ☐	11. ☐
12. Increase Annual Acquisitions by 20%	$ +160,000	12. ☐	12. ☐	12. ☐
13. Decrease Annual Acquisitions by 10%	$ −80,000	13. ☐	13. ☐	13. ☐
14. Decrease Annual Acquisitions by 20%	$ −160,000	14. ☐	14. ☐	14. ☐
15. Limited Cataloging	$ −75,000	15. ☐	15. ☐	15. ☐
16. Cut Reference Staff by 10%	$ −25,000	16. ☐	16. ☐	16. ☐
17. Add to Reference Staff by 10%	$ +25,000	17. ☐	17. ☐	17. ☐
18. Improved Access to Another Collection, say Wellesley	$ +30,000	18. ☐	18. ☐	18. ☐
19. Library of Congress Messenger Service	$ +10,000	19. ☐	19. ☐	19. ☐
20. Additional Copies of 1/2 of Reserve Books	$ +50,000	20. ☐	20. ☐	20. ☐

Figure 12   (Continued)

No._____

BACKGROUND DATA

1. M.I.T. Status
       _____(1) Freshman
       _____(2) Sophomore
       _____(3) Junior
       _____(4) Senior
       _____(5) Graduate Student (Masters)
       _____(6) Graduate Student (Ph.D.—
             not on theses)
       _____(7) Graduate Student (Ph.D.—
             on thesis)
       _____(8) Faculty
       _____(9) D.S.R.
       _____(10) Other   (Specify)_____

2. Course or Department
   Number_____

3. Residence

   _____(1) Dormitory
   _____(2) Off-Campus
            Living Group

   _____(3) Private Residence

4. Of the possible functions or roles of the libraries listed below, check those functions that are most significant to you.
       _____To provide the means to discover and/or browse through new books
       _____To provide the means to browse and read current journals
       _____To provide an informal place to lounge, relax, and socialize
       _____To provide required and recommended reading
       _____To provide a *place* to study required and recommended reading
       _____To provide a *place* to study your own material
       _____To provide books and material for research and term papers
       _____To provide bibliographic services
       _____To provide reference aids through professional librarians
       _____Other (please specify)_____

5. About how many hours do you spend during a typical week in any of the M.I.T. libraries (Aero, Astro, Dewey, Engineering, Humanities, Lindgren, Science or Student Center)? Check one.
       _____(1) 0–5 hours per week
       _____(2) 6–10 hours per week
       _____(3) 11–15 hours per week
       _____(4) 16–20 hours per week
       _____(5) 21–25 hours per week
       _____(6) 26–30 hours per week
       _____(7) more than 30 hours per week

6. How much money do you spend each year on books for academic purposes?
          $_____

7. How much money do you spend each year on course required or recommended books?
   $_____

Figure 12   (Continued)

therefore the conclusions below should be read with some skepticism as to absolute responses.

A second concern is that people cannot visualize systems with which they have not had direct experience. It could be argued that the written descriptions of benefits are not adequate for individuals to make valid decisions. It must be noted that no system on the list deviated greatly from current technology or systems; most called for enlarging or restructuring current services. For example, some departments charge less for making Xerox copies, some professors do hand out Xeroxed copies of papers or articles as in the all-Xerox reserve alternative, and departmental libraries of varying nature do exist. Furthermore, although it is of course possible that non-respondents had difficulty with the survey and thus did not return it, only one respondent questioned the amount of information provided for decisions; yet he dutifully filled out the questionnaire. Similarly, over 20 pretest respondents who filled out the questionnaire said that they felt the comparisons were meaningful to them.

A further problem involves the complexity of the task, and one may question if respondents could answer rationally. As a test of the degree to which people did understand the decisions to be made, "rationality" was checked by comparing the responses at different budget levels. For many of the systems, e.g., increased acquisitions, if respondents were "rational," their choices should be patterned so that if a system with a positive cost is chosen at the $0 or $100,000 budget level it will be chosen at higher budget levels.[8]

Table 17 shows that the systems did not differ significantly in rank from one budget level to the next. The last check was the number of respondents who filled out only one column and thus did not follow the directions. Less than 5% made this mistake.

A more crucial problem, and one which cannot be solved, is whether the respondents chose a system because of its value to themselves, as they were instructed, or because of the perceived value of the system to M.I.T. The responses appear consistent with the former reason, at least in terms of subgroup selection patterns. For example, in a decision of apparent self-interest, students do select an all-Xerox reserve system much more frequently than faculty members.

---

[8]This is equivalent in economic theory to the assumption that many of the systems are *superior* or *neutral goods*.

Table 17.   Preference Rankings by Budget Levels

	Budget Levels		
Positive Cost Systems	$200,000	$100,000	$0
Increase acquisitions	1*	2	2
Lower Xerox rates	2	1	1
LC messenger	3	3	3
Expand seating	4	4	4
Add reserve copies	5	5	4
Add reference	6	7	6
Increase access	7	6	7
Departmental libraries	8	9	9
All-Xerox reserve	9	8	8
Negative Cost Systems			
Centralize reserve	1*	1	1
Inexpensive storage	2	2	2
Cut reference	3	3	4
Cut seating	4	4	3
Decrease acquisitions	5	5	5

*Rank of system where rank of 1 means the system was chosen the most at that budget level.

A more basic question involves the meaning of the responses to those responsible for allocating library funds. What role can such a benefit survey play in library decision-making? First, this survey gives an indication of the systems all members of the M.I.T. community would like to have. Second, the number of people supporting or vociferously opposing certain systems may be determined. The decrease in the popularity of a positive cost system as the budget level decreases may be a measure of the intensity of feeling, if any, for that system. Thus those items vigorously supported by a minority may be located. Few librarians feel comfortable basing their decisions only on the vocalized fears of a few concerned faculty members. Third, the inclusion of costs as a decision criterion eliminates the necessity of speculating (by the respondent or the decision-maker) as to whether individuals would continue to support a given system if "they knew what it cost." Fourth, the survey can provide librarians with information to permit them to encourage the use of the library and to support library programs which they feel are educationally superior. Variables have been specified, for example, which are related to seeing the library as a place to study one's own material. Would librarians like to change these factors to discourage (or encourage) such use?

The key point comes last. What role should the desires of students play in the university allocational process? Should a library be run by public opinion? If one believes that the preferences of students should not "interfere" with the educational decision process then the survey (or at least the responses of students) is of limited value. If one believes that surveys are not sufficient substitutes for a direct political role for students in university decision-making, then, again, the survey is of limited value.

Results: Absolute Preferences

Table 18 lists the percentage of respondents selecting each system at each of the three budget levels. The pairs of alternatives for increasing acquisitions, expanding seating, altering book stacks or storage, and cutting seating are combined within brackets.

Table 18.   Percentages of Respondents Choosing System by Budget Level*

System	Budget Level		
	$200,000	$100,000	$0
[Increase acquisitions, 10% or 20%]	[78%]	[61%]	[41%]
Lower Xerox rates	74	65	54
LC messenger service	55	44	32
[Expand seating, 10% or 20%]	[48]	[32]	[16]
Add reserve copies	43	28	18
Increase acquisitions, 20%	43	8	4
Centralize reserve	41	48	62
Increase acquisitions, 10%	35	53	37
Add reference librarians	33	19	13
Expand seating, 10%	31	23	12
Increase access to other libraries	30	23	12
Departmental libraries	28	16	6
All-Xerox reserve	27	17	8
[Conventional or compact storage]	[24]	[24]	[34]
Expand seating, 20%	17	9	4
Conventional storage	16	16	21
[Cut seating, 10% or 20%]	[11]	[14]	[24]
Cut reference staff	10	16	20
Limit cataloging	8	12	17
Compact storage	8	8	13
Cut seating, 10%	8	10	12
Cut seating, 20%	3	4	12
Decrease acquisitions, 10%	0	0	3
Decrease acquisitions, 20%	0	0	0

*Related pairs of alternatives are combined within brackets.

About three quarters of the respondents (74%) desired lower Xerox rates at the highest budget level. This selection rate decreases to 54% at the present (or $0 supplemental) budget level, but this decrease is proportionally less than for other popular systems. For example, the number selecting alternatives to increase acquisitions decreases by 50% across the budget levels. It is assumed that this sharp drop indicates a relative lack of intensity on the part of respondents for increased acquisitions as compared to lowering Xerox rates. Those who no longer select an alternative at the lowest budget level, i.e., where additional money is not available, are not as concerned with having the system as those who have given up other systems to retain the alternative. Since the instructions permitted respondents to spend $15,000 over the budget level (or under), lower Xerox prices could have been selected at no "expense," i.e., without giving up other systems at the $0 budget level. Approximately twenty people did this, not enough to warrant a different conclusion about intensity.[9]

While respondents were attracted to lower Xerox rates, few desired an all-Xerox reserve system. About a quarter (27%) chose this alternative at the highest budget level. Thus respondents preferred the less costly and more flexible Xerox system to the more limited reserve Xerox system. A few commented that the lower prices would be unnecessary if reserve items were permitted to circulate, allowing users to take advantage of lower departmental prices. The survey indicates, however, that support for lower prices extends beyond those with access to departmental Xeroxing. A majority (54%) would alter the current library to permit the adoption of lower Xerox prices.

Even stronger than the desire for increased acquisitions was the reluctance to decrease acquisitions. The 3% of the people at the $0 budget level who called for decreasing acquisitions by 10% were the exceptions. In comparison, 24% chose to reduce seating at this same budget level. At this budget level, almost half (41%) were willing to save money to increase acquisitions, but the vast majority of these people (37% of the 41%) desired a 10% rather than a 20% increase. One concludes that increased acquisitions are desired by those at

[9]It was also possible that people tended to select the lower cost systems because of their costs rather than their total merits. It was not possible to determine whether respondents used only costs rather than costs and benefits as a decision criterion. Although there was an association between the cost of an alternative and its being selected, systems with the same cost did differ considerably in popularity. For example, adding reserve copies and expanding seating 20% both cost $50,000, yet the latter ranked eleventh in popularity at the $200,000 budget level. Only two of five such comparisons indicated a cost-popularity similarity, thus strengthening our conclusion that more than costs were considered. (Appendix 13 reports the cost and popularity ranks for all positive cost systems.)

M.I.T. given more library funds, but few are in favor of drastically altering the current library to purchase a greater number of books.

The Library of Congress messenger service was a popular item, retaining support even at the $0 budget level.[10]   Access to other university libraries was less popular in approximate proportion to its added cost ($10,000 vs. $30,000).   There were few advocates of departmental libraries or all-Xerox reserve.   Although about half of the respondents (48%) called for expanded seating at the highest budget level, only one third of these respondents selected either of these alternatives at the lowest budget level.   Increased seating was less salient or desired than increased acquisitions.   This suggests that seating may be a service which could be altered to meet rising demands for space or funds without upsetting too many people.

There was great agreement on the most preferred way to save money to purchase alternative systems.   Over 40% of the respondents desired a centralized reserve system even at the $200,000 budget level.   Although it was not tested, it could well be that many (especially undergraduates) would have selected centralized reserve even if it had a positive cost.   The less expensive storage alternatives were moderately popular as money-saving alternatives, yet those who were opposed to these systems were strongly opposed.   The number choosing these alternatives is relatively insensitive to changes in the budget level.   The same percentage of respondents, for example, selects an inexpensive storage system even where the supplemental budget is doubled from $100,000 to $200,000.   Moreover, many respondents wrote spontaneous comments such as "never" or "don't do it" near this system description on the answer sheet.   It appears that book storage savings are preferred to seating cuts by those who sought to save money.   Yet those who were against seating cuts at the higher budget levels did not appear to be as intent against cutting seating at lower levels.   They were more flexible in comparison to those opposed to storage changes.   How can librarians choose between an intense minority who are against any stack alteration and perhaps a near majority who are less intense but would prefer to alter storage rather than seating?   Although political theorists have debated this question for centuries, the

[10]The Library of Congress messenger service is not necessarily a feasible system, given political realities (e.g., what if all major libraries adopted such a system?). Yet, the preference for the LC system gives one an indication of a desire to expand the M.I.T. collection by increasing access to very large libraries. It is not an argument for immediately adopting such a system without other considerations.

librarian's solution may well be to ignore both and to centralize the reserve system.[11]

It should be noted that decreasing the reference staff and limiting cataloging were not more popular than the more conventional solutions to the money or space shortage problem.

Results: Response Patterns

Response patterns, i.e., regularities in the alternatives chosen by individuals, are useful because (a) they indicate overall orientations toward different aspects of the library so that one can predict which people will respond in different ways to a given innovation, (b) they allow the analyst to rank individuals on a single dimension or to take responses to a single alternative as an indicator of preferences, and (c) they indicate what systems serve as substitutes for one another or are seen as incompatible by respondents.

Appendix 14 summarizes the relations between each pair of systems at the $200,000 budget level. The measure of association used was Kendall's Q, and the reader is warned that no absolute meaning may be given to these numbers. The association measure ranges from -1 to $+1$ where 0 indicates no relation. A Q of 0.8 shows more association than a Q of 0.4, but it cannot be interpreted as being twice as much. The table is presented as being suggestive, and the conclusions drawn were made from a qualitative rather than a quantitative pattern analysis, the latter being inappropriate to nominal data.

Two general orientations are evident. One is a "research orientation"; but the second is not a reserve or course orientation as was expected, but rather an orientation that has been labeled an "outside use orientation."[12] The latter orientation is suggested by the cluster of alternatives which tended to be chosen together. Figure 13 indicates the association between the four basic components of this orientation. (Note that the other seating alternatives fit the same pattern, but were excluded for simplicity.) The lack of association between the all-Xerox reserve and additional reserve copies indicates that either may be part of the orientation but both are not necessarily selected by those with the outside use orientation. People who choose one reserve alternative are not much more likely to choose

[11]See again Kendall and Carey, Downs, and Arrow for a discussion of aggregating responses to determine a social welfare function (Footnote 4).

[12]"Outside use" refers to using library materials outside of the library.

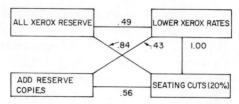

Figure 13. Association among "outside-use orientation" systems. Numbers are Q-measure of association.

the other alternative, but those who choose one of the four components are likely to choose the others. The factor has been labeled "outside use orientation," because the emphasis is primarily on making it easier to use library books or to copy library materials for use outside the library and to save money on facilities necessary for use in the library. This finding supports a view of the library as a dispenser of materials, and as a facilitator of communication, rather than as a place to work. It lends support to efforts of those who support making the dormitory room a more attractive place to study and the library as an adjunct to the bookstore.

The other orientation is a "research orientation." (See Figure 14.) The pattern consists of selecting increased acquisitions, the LC mes-

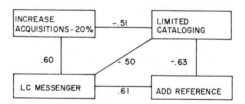

Figure 14. Association among "research orientation" systems. Numbers are Q-measure of association.

senger service, improved access to other libraries, and more reference staff, and not selecting limited cataloging or a reduced reference staff. The components thus are (a) improving access to other collections, (b) increasing M.I.T.'s collection, and (c) improving or maintaining in-house library services. Note that improving acquisitions is not associated with adding reserve copies. This indicates that respondents did not want just to add books but rather general collection books. Increased acquisitions was highly correlated with selecting departmental libraries. The term "departmental libraries" is usually associated with research and journal-oriented libraries; thus, although departmental library selection was not related to all the other components, it did appear to be linked to a research orientation. One interpretation could be that those who selected departmental libraries are oriented toward journals rather than research per se. This is consistent with the positive association (Q = 0.42) between selecting limited cataloging (which would not affect journals) and departmental libraries. In the research orientation pattern, this association was reversed. This would add support to arguments for increasing departmental libraries limited to current journals rather than those which would include research books or papers.

This brief analysis of the patterns of responses should not lead the reader to conclude that there are only two types of potential library users. The two types are pure types; most respondents did not select the entire set of alternatives of one orientation while ignoring the other. These types do suggest, however, a re-examination of the dispensing functions of the library, particularly with respect to Xeroxing and paperback copies of popular books.

Results: Subgroup Analysis

Table 19 summarizes the percentages of respondents choosing the alternative systems by their M.I.T. status. Most of the patterns are

Table 19.   System Preferences by M.I.T. Status at $200,000 Budget Level

System	M.I.T. Status		
	Undergraduates	Graduates	Faculty and DSR*
Inexpensive storage systems	24%	16%	33%
Expand seating, 10% or 20%	47	55	45
Cut seating, 10% or 20%	8	14	11
Centralized reserve	49	46	30
Lower Xerox rates	67	85	76
Departmental libraries	21	19	49
All-Xerox reserve	42	21	14
Increase acquisitions, 10% or 20%	78	90	73
Limited cataloging	11	4	10
Cut reference	11	13	5
Add reference	30	51	36
Increased access to other libraries	31	39	22
LC messenger service	58	61	48
Add reserve copies	53	49	27

*Division of Sponsored Research.

consistent with our initial expectations. Undergraduates are more likely to select systems which alter or augment the reserve system (primarily, increased copies for reserve, all-Xerox reserve, and centralizing reserve) and more willing to change library research facilities and services (primarily, inexpensive storage systems, more limited cataloging, and a decreased reference staff). In general undergraduates appear to want to shift funds from research to reserve. The absolute responses at the $0 budget level indicate that although they disagree on the system on which to spend the savings, about three-quarters (70%) of the undergraduates surveyed desired to centralize the reserve system.

Graduate students display a different pattern. Like undergraduates, they favor (relative to the faculty) centralized reserve and increased acquisitions, but they also want increased access to the collections of other universities and the Library of Congress and lower Xerox rates. They are also more reluctant to alter research aids such as storage or cataloging. At the $0 budget level, a majority favor centralized reserve (64%), a majority desire lower Xerox prices (58%), and slightly less want to increase acquisitions. (See Table 20.)

Table 20.   System Preferences by M.I.T. Status at $0 Budget Level

System	M.I.T. Status		
	Undergraduates	Graduates	Faculty and DSR
Inexpensive storage systems	34%	31%	38%
Expand seating, 10% or 20%	23	9	16
Cut seating, 10% or 20%	22	31	17
Centralized reserve	70	64	52
Lower Xerox rates	53	58	52
Departmental libraries	3	1	14
All-Xerox reserve	10	10	3
Increase acquisitions, 10% or 20%	45	49	28
Limited cataloging	20	10	22
Cut reference	24	25	8
Add reference	13	16	10
Increased access to other libraries	13	12	8
LC messenger	44	25	24
Add reserve copies	21	16	13

Surprisingly, the faculty respondents are more likely than students to favor inexpensive storage systems, although at the $0 budget level less than 40 percent (38%) favor either system. They are also more willing to limit cataloging than students. Their relative unwillingness to support a centralized reserve system may be a lack of knowledge or interest rather than self-interest opposition, although this can be only a tentative conclusion. The faculty are the primary supporters of departmental libraries.

The general conclusion is that the three major campus groups differ in the systems they would like the library to adopt. Undergraduates seek to expand and centralize the reserve collection by cutting research services. Graduate students add lower Xerox prices and increased access to this list of desired systems and would prefer to cut seating rather than cataloging. The faculty are the most willing to alter book storage and cataloging and relatively less desirous of a centralized reserve system.

Respondents were divided into three groups by the number of weekly hours they reported using the M.I.T. libraries. The "lows" reported using them 0 to 5 hours per week, the "moderates" between 5 and 10 hours, and the "highs" 10 hours or more. The mode or most chosen response, it should be noted, was a "low" response.

The less a respondent reported using the libraries the more likely he was to select saving money on book storage and seating and to spend it on lower Xerox rates, departmental libraries, and an all-Xerox reserve system. Low users thus tend to be outside-use oriented. The high users prefer expanding seating, acquisitions, reference, and access to other collections. The high users thus are research oriented. We have concluded that the library has traditionally served one clientele, the research oriented. There now appears to be, however, a second clientele, who spend few hours in the library and seek not the space but the materials in its collection. We believe, with as yet no proof, that many of those oriented to outside use prefer to work outside the library but are forced, primarily by the reserve system, to work in the library. We hypothesize that these users (and many other potential users) could be served by a library emphasizing distribution as well as in-house facilities and services.

Respondents were also grouped by their department or major field into three categories: science, engineering, and other (primarily, humanities, social science, and management). As illustrated in Table 21, there was no strong relation or pattern of relations between a respondent's field and his preference at the $200,000 budget level. For example, it was hypothesized that those in the nontechnical fields would be more likely to want increased access to other collections and increased M.I.T. acquisitions to overcome the inadequacies of M.I.T.'s nontechnical collection. The differences among the three fields are insignificant.

Table 21.   Field by Preferences at the $200,000 Budget Level

Field	Percentage Selecting System			
	Either Inexpensive Storage	Lower Xerox Rates	Increase Acquisitions, 20%	Increase Access
Engineering (100)	19%	85%	38%	30%
Science (98)	15	72	42	29
Other (81)	16	75	42	30

Respondents were also asked what to them were the most significant purposes of the library. Table 22 summarizes the responses. Although this question was intended to serve as an intervening variable between status and preferences, the overall responses to this question proved to be more interesting. Few respondents view the library as a *place* to study either their own or the library's material. The results also suggest that those who see the library as a place to study library material may prefer not to study there. Those who see the library as a place to study required reading are *more* likely to want more reserve copies (56% to 27%). Although one may interpret this preference as a concern for just more copies and thus a greater chance to obtain a book at any given moment, we believe that most respondents saw the added copies as a way to take out books and thus leave the library. When these responses are compared to the majority of preferences, which are related more to providing materials than to providing a place to use the materials, two of the earlier conclusions are given added support: first, that there is a strong feeling that the library should be a provider of materials and should encourage users to read materials elsewhere; second, a closely related proposition that people are less concerned with seating than with borrowing books and browsing.

Table 22.   Main Purposes of Library to Respondents*

Provide books and material for research	76%
Provide means to browse and read current journals	63
Provide required and recommended reading	61
Provide means to browse and read new books	43
Provide reference aids through professional libraries	29
Provide bibliographic services	27
Provide a place to study required and recommended reading	22
Provide a place to study your own material	20
Other	6
Provide informal place to lounge, relax, socialize	2

*Respondents were permitted to choose as many responses as they wished.

A respondent's choice of the major purposes of the library to him is not highly related to his choice of systems (Table 23). The exception is the choice of 20% increased acquisitions. Those who see the library's purpose in terms of providing course materials and new books are more likely to select increased acquisitions than those who see the library as a place to study, to browse through journals, and to obtain reference help. Yet this pattern does not hold for any other system, and one must conclude that neither a respondent's department or perception of the purpose of the library influence a respondent's preference for library systems as does his M.I.T. status.

Table 23. Perceived Purposes of Library by Preferences at $200,000 Budget Level

Perceived Purpose of Library to Respondent	Percentage Preferring Each System			
	Either Expensive Seating System	Lower Xerox Prices	Increase Acquisitions 20%	Increase Access
Provide means to browse and read current journals (177)	25%	77%	41%	27%
Provide required and recommended reading (171)	26	77	56	33
Provide means to browse and read new books (125)	21	66	66	23
Provide reference aids through professional librarians (82)	27	78	40	32
Provide a place to study required and recommended reading (64)	21	71	34	28

Conclusion

The benefit survey has thus indicated that the library should use current reproduction technology and paperback books to encourage people to use library materials outside the library. There is also a strong preference for centralizing the reserve collections. Most significantly, the survey substantiated the hypothesis that different members of the M.I.T. community are satisfied by different allocations of the M.I.T. library budget.

6 Conclusions

Major Findings

A. Programming Planning Budgeting System
 1. It is feasible to develop a meaningful program budget for library operations through time surveys, floor-space allocations, etc., and to determine annual expenditures by output categories.
 2. The M.I.T. libraries presently spend about three-quarters of their annual resources (est. $2,280,000) to provide a general and research collection and the remaining one-quarter to provide required reading and course-related study facilities.
    a. Cataloging and book purchasing are both substantial portions of the total library budget with cataloging (17.3%) consuming even more than purchasing (16.7%).
    b. Total floor-space costs account for almost 20% of the total annual expenditures.
       (1) The libraries spend 50% more "storing" people in seats than storing books in stacks (11.4% vs. 7.4% of the total annual expenditures).
       (2) Providing desk and lounge space is the most significant cost factor of the study-related library expenses (37.4%).
B. Storage
 1. Altering the current storage system is not a very satisfactory way to save money. The best alternative system, compact storage, saves only about 15% of the current library expenditures on the storage of nonreserve books, while storage expenditures for nonreserve books are only 6.4% of the annual budget. The saving, about 1% of annual library resources (less, if expensive retrieval systems are necessary), involves

68

a major loss of benefits because of limitations on browsing and retrieval delay times of perhaps several hours.

a. Neither location (on vs. off campus) nor access mode (closed vs. open access) affects significantly the cost of storing books.

b. For collections characterized by "moderate use," storing books compactly instead of conventionally reduces the annual per volume storage cost by 50%, from about $.28 to about $.14.

c. However, because of the necessity to weed the collection periodically and perhaps to provide a retrieval system, the net saving due to compact storage reduces the annual per volume cost by only 10 to 20%.

    (1) The publication-date weeding criterion is more cost-effective for the Dewey library collection than the circulation criterion.

    (2) Compact storage facilities should be placed within fast walking distance of the circulation desks to allow regular library personnel to retrieve books, thus eliminating the need for expensive motorized systems.

2. Microform storage is appropriate only for material which does not have to be converted into microform.

a. With current technology the cost of converting a 400-page book is about $8.

b. Where microform facsimiles are initially available, the attractiveness of the microform storage system depends heavily on the number and type of readers and reader printers.

C. Study Facilities

1. There is a wide interlibrary variation (up to a factor of 2) in the cost of providing the same kind of seat.

2. The cost of seating varies because of the various degrees to which economies of scale and economies of planning are applied.

3. Lounge seating is expensive not because of the cost of furniture but because of the large cost of the required floor space.

4. Classrooms, dining halls, and other areas adjacent to libraries could be operated as additional library study space during peak hours as an alternative to more studying facilities within the libraries.

5. Linear programming can be used to analyze and suboptimize seating requirements in the library.

D. Reserve

1. The current reserve system could be vastly improved by a 10 to 20% increase in that component of the program budget.

   a. Xerox copying should be used as a part of the library instead of an extra-cost service.

   b. Xerox charges should be competitive with local commercial rates to encourage students to reproduce and remove copies of journal articles, reserve articles, etc., rather than to occupy library seats.

   c. A better alternative than the use of microform systems for reserve is a Xerox system in which reproduced articles are distributed to students.

2. At present, students spend 50% more than the libraries for course-related study material.

   a. About $1,350,000 is spent annually to provide required reading to students.

   b. A reasonable estimate of what students think they spend on course-required and recommended reading per student per year is $100, thus totaling about $720,000 for the M.I.T. student body.

E. Cataloging

1. The major cataloging expenses are for cataloging items by professional librarians ($98,250 annually) and for proofreading and checking catalog cards ($46,000 annually).

   a. Limited cataloging appears to offer the possibility of large savings; but

   b. Temporary cataloging appears to offer little or no savings.

2. Computerized catalogs may be "even better than we think" since they would allow:

   a. Decentralized catalogs on campus which could be combined with fast messenger services;

   b. Cooperative acquisition agreements with other nearby university libraries, and

   c. Common access to other collections that were "tied in" to the system.

3. Microform catalogs are extremely expensive even without considering the high cost of making changes and additions.

F. Selection and Acquisition

1. To continue current selection policies, acquisition funds will have to double within the next six to eight years.

2. Extrapolation of recent publishing and price trends seems to indicate that it will be relatively more costly to maintain an up-to-date science and technology collection than an up-to-date social science collection.

3. It would seem possible to secure the current number of significant uses at lower cost by shifting money from purchasing/processing into selection, since a certain portion of books purchased will rarely, if ever, be used.

4. A common acquisitions policy with Wellesley, as well as commonality of user services and privileges, appears to be a relatively inexpensive way of truly complementing the current library holdings.

G. Ordering and Supplemental Retrieval Systems

1. Marginal journals should be ordered on commercial microfilm, if available, at the year's end.

2. Interlibrary loan should be looked at as an alternative to purchasing marginal books, and, as such, should be expanded by cooperative agreement with other schools to increase internal efficiency.

3. A Library of Congress retrieval system, were it acceptable to the Library of Congress, may not be any more expensive per request fulfilled than the current interlibrary loan service.

H. Measuring Benefits: General Methodological Conclusions

1. Survey research, despite its limitations, is useful in aiding decision-makers to solve problems of benefit measurement.

2. User surveys which also survey all potential users and provide respondents with cost information about alternatives may provide new insights into the preferences of students and faculty.

I. Measuring Benefits: Results of the Benefit Survey

1. There is a general orientation toward increasing the library's role as a distributor of materials for use outside the library. A majority of students and faculty would alter the present library in order to save money so that lower Xerox prices could be adopted.

2. There is a "research orientation," and related to this orientation is strong support for marginal increases in acquisitions at the expense of other systems. Few desire a radical increase in acquisitions (i.e., 20%) at the present budget level, and virtually no one wants to decrease acquisitions to adopt any other system. Given more funds, however, a large increase in acquisitions is highly popular.

3. Centralizing the reserve libraries appears to be very popular, especially among those who presumably would be most affected, i.e., students rather than faculty.
4. Feelings against inexpensive storage systems run high, yet about one-third would be willing to adopt one of the systems at the present budget level. Seating changes, although less popular as a means of saving money, are also less *unpopular* (i.e., provokes less intense feelings) and may be a superior means of saving money or space. Neither changing reference personnel nor changing cataloging proved popular.
5. Different groups at M.I.T. prefer different budget allocations. Undergraduates tend to prefer shifting funds from research to reserve; graduate students are more outside-use oriented (they especially want lower Xerox prices) and desire increased access to other collections; the faculty (49% at the $200,000 budget level) seek departmental libraries. Surprisingly enough, perhaps because of indifference, the faculty are more likely to support inexpensive book storage.
6. Infrequent users of the library (in terms of hours spent weekly in the library) tend to be the most outside-use oriented and high users are research oriented. The library appears now to be oriented toward the latter group.
7. Since there is no relation among major field or department and system preferences, it does not appear that those in the social sciences or humanities are any more dissatisfied than those in engineering and science or that they seek a different basic library. As the number of nontechnical students and faculty rises, there is no indication that the basic nature of the library would have to be altered. The distribution of faculty, undergraduates, and graduate students is more significant.

Future Research Questions

The following additional research areas should also be examined in evaluating future library systems:

A. Selection
   1. Relation between selection expenses and benefits.
   2. Extent to which circulations measure the value of a book.
   3. Cost and benefits of faculty selection systems.
   4. Possibility of cooperation in acquisitions with local universities.

B. Cataloging
   1. Loss in benefits and decrease in costs associated with "limited" cataloging.
   2. Augmented catalogs (Project INTREX).
C. User Behavior
   1. Seating preferences and seating behavior.
   2. Frequency of serendipitous activities.
   3. Use of Xerox and Xeroxed materials throughout M.I.T.—study of Xerox system.
   4. Frequency and types of browsing.
D. Collection Description
   1. Variation across libraries and fields by use and age.
E. Miscellaneous
   1. Reliability of personnel costs—Fall or Spring survey.
   2. Additional benefit studies.
   3. Possibility of combining graduate lounges, study rooms.
   4. Bookstore subsidization or incorporation with the library.
   5. Economies of scale in seating arrangements.
   6. Student expenditures on course-required or recommended material—the "community budget."

Appendix 1   Personnel Time Survey

Library Function

A. *Selection of books, pamphlets, etc., for acquisition*
   1. Processing recommendations, selecting tentative list of books to be ordered.
   2. Checking catalogs to see if book is already ordered or in the collection.
   3. Other (please specify)
B. *Ordering of books, pamphlets, etc.*
   1. Combining order lists, writing orders to publisher or jobbers, receiving and recording incoming books, claiming missing titles.
   2. Changing order lists (or catalog) and collection catalog.
   3. Other
C. *Cataloging*
   1. Searching for Library of Congress catalog card.
   2. Classifying (i.e., cataloging) non-Library of Congress book, pamphlet, etc.
   3. Typing catalog card or card additions.
   4. Proofreading catalog cards, checking catalog.
   5. Placing cards in catalog.
   6. LC cataloging.
   7. Other
D. *Preparation and Binding*
   1. Books, reports, pamphlets—bookmarking of ownership, date received, pocketing, jacketing, call number placement.
   2. Periodicals
      a. Binding.
      b. Rebinding and repairing.
   3. Books, reports, other nonperiodicals—rebinding and repairing.
   4. Other
E. *Circulation*
   1. Shelving

      a. New books.
      b. Returns—taken out of library.
      c. Returns—in library circulation.
      d. Misplaced, errant.
   2. Recording books to be taken out (date, etc.).
   3. Finding and notifying delinquents.
   4. Theft and circulation checking.
   5. Interlibrary loan.
      a. Lending
      b. Borrowing
   6. Removal—weeding, storage, disposal.
   7. Other

F. *Reference and Information*
   1. Forming bibliographies, abstracting, making indexes, and selected lists.
   2. Intermediate inquiries (answer wanted on the spot).
      a. Catalog aid or search.
      b. Equipment instruction.
      c. Search for specific book.
      d. Search for specific information.
      e. Library instruction.
   3. Delayed inquiries (those not urgent rather than delayed by necessity—say when lacking material for reply).
   4. Other

G. *Reserve*
   1. Collecting, collating lists of required reading from professors.
   2. Searching out books, reports, etc., needed, checking if already on reserve.
   3. Reproducing reserve materials (done by your library or department).
   4. Setting up reserve catalog or listing.
   5. Information—answering inquiries.
   6. Maintaining shelves.
   7. Returning books to general collection.
   8. Circulation—checking out books, theft control.
   9. Other

H. *Supervision*
   1. Available for emergencies, information, but not engaged actively in work (as an example, sitting at desk in reserve room waiting to be asked any questions that arise).

I. *Reproduction*
   1. Giving instructions on using machines.

2. Reproducing materials for students, faculty, guests.
3. Reproducing material for library (other than for reserve).
   a. Catalog cards
   b. Other
4. Other

J . *Other*—Please try to match your time with the above descriptions. However, if you perform an activity that has not been listed, please describe here and indicate.

1. Straightening up desks.
2. Reading shelves.
3. Working on mail.
4. Working on invoices.
5. Messenger

How would you describe your activities yesterday?

_____Very typical for the summer months
_____ Typical for the summer months
_____ Not typical for the summer months
_____ Extraordinary for the summer months
_____ Don't know

If you have answered *not typical, extraordinary,* or *don't know,* please indicate why and how your time estimates would differ.

Summary of Results	
Very typical and typical	62%
Not typical	12
Don't know	8
No answer	18
$N = 83$	

Appendix 2   Program Budget—1966 to 1967

	Processing	Library Divisions	General Library Admin.
Research and General Collection			
A. Collection building:			
Selection of items to be ordered for collection	$ 7,125	$ 49,250	$ 5,800
Ordering of items from publishers, jobber	49,600	84,000	14,900
Purchase costs of—(a) Books, monographs	0	0	0
(b) Serials	0	0	0
(c) Journals	0	0	0
Cataloging items (a) Using Library of Congress card	88,800	26,250	11,500
(b) Original cataloging	130,200	18,560	14,900
(c) Recataloging	19,400	14,900	6,900
New item preparation (bookmarking, etc.) and distribution to divisional libraries	32,800	5,980	3,100
B. Collection maintenance:			
Stacks	0	0	0
Item repair, rebinding	11,900	7,460	1,770
Binding of serials, journals	7,300	8,710	1,440
C. User services:			
Research reading desks (25% of total)	0	0	0
Circulation	32,400	130,000	16,100
Interlibrary loan and borrowing	0	18,000	1,690
Information and bibliographic aid	4,400	196,000	20,000
Required Reading and Studying			
A. Collection building:			
Purchasing (books)	0	0	0
Processing (selection, ordering, preparation)	4,775	7,450	0
Xeroxing	0	0	0
Cataloging (added copies)	19,400	14,900	0
B. Collection maintenance:			
Stacks, desks, general	0	0	0
C. User services:			
General services, information aid, circulation	25,175	112,000	13,700
Study spaces (75% of total)	0	0	0
Research and Development (Technical Information Program	56,340	0	0

Jobber Costs	Purchase Supply Costs	Floor Space Costs	Total Annual Costs	Percent of Total Budget	
$0	$ 6,000	$ 8,060	$ 76,235	3.3	
0	6,000	11,900	166,400	7.3	
0	168,000	0	168,000	7.4	
0	39,265	0	39,265	1.7	
0	91,116	0	91,116	4.0	
0	6,900	3,120	136,570	6.0	
0	5,200	3,120	171,980	7.5	
0	3,950	1,560	46,710	2.1	
5,950	6,820	2,340	56,990	2.5	
					Subtotal 41.8%
0	0	144,800	144,800	6.4	
5,513	6,225	1,900	34,768	1.5	
28,028	6,225	1,700	53,403	2.3	
					Subtotal 10.2%
0	0	64,800	64,800	2.8	
0	2,275	3,280	184,055	8.1	
0	1,540	0	21,230	1.0	
0	0	0	220,400	9.8	
					Subtotal 21.7%
0	81,200	0	81,200	3.6	
300	1,005	1,110	14,640	.6	
0	18,000	0	18,000	.8	
0	3,950	1,560	39,810	1.7	
					Subtotal 6.7%
0	0	25,000	25,000	1.0	
					Subtotal 1.0%
0	2,275	0	153,150	6.7	
0	0	196,300	196,300	8.6	
					Subtotal 15.3%
0	11,500	6,800	74,640	3.3	
			$2,279,572	100.0%	Subtotal 3.3%

Appendix 3   Floor Space in Square Feet

Divisions of Floor Space	Dewey-Rotch-Aero	Stu. Ctr.	Lind-gren	Engr.	Hayden	Res. Room
Selection	615	200	50	50	1500	—
Ordering	1500	200	50	50	1500	—
Purchasing	—	—	—	—	—	—
Cataloging (divided evenly):						
(a) LC card	250	—	25	50	500	—
(b) Original cat.	250	—	25	50	500	—
(c) Recat.	250	—	25	50	500	—
Preparation	250	200	—	—	200	—
Distribution	—	—	—	—	—	—
Stacks	7100	—	980	15200	17220	—
Repairing	250	—	—	50	200	—
Binding	250	—	—	—	200	—
Circulation:						
(a) Reserve	1225	600	—	—	3720	1040
(b) Nonreserve	460	—	100	100	200	—
(c) Interlibrary	—	—	—	—	—	—
Study (includes lounges, tables)	15600	19000	3240	4100	21600	700
Copying	250	—	—	50	3400	—
Information	—	—	—	—	—	—
General Adminis-tration	2600	—	225	350	1620	—
Technical Information Processing	—	—	—	—	1800	—
TOTAL	30850	20200	4720	20100	54660	1740

Appendix 4   Cost Per Item—From M.I.T. Program Budget

	Total Annual Cost	Total Number Books, Serials, etc.	Cost/Item
Processing			
Selection	$ 76,235	49,656	$ 1.54
Ordering	166,400	49,656	3.35
Preparation (bookmarking, etc.)	56,990	95,661	.60
Cataloging with LC card	136,570	14,421	9.47
Cataloging without LC card	160,000*	10,885	14.70
Cataloging additional copies	46,710	8,231	5.67
Purchasing			
Monographs (books, pamphlets, slices)	168,000	39,660	4.24
Serials	39,265	4,601	8.53
Journals	91,116	5,234	17.40

Storing the Collection

Total number of volumes (including books, slides, serials, etc.)	= 1,155,480
Total cost per year	= $144,800
Cost per volume per year	= $.12

User Services

Nonreserve circulations	= 167,575
Total cost per year	= $184,055
Cost per nonreserve circulation	= $1.10
Information and bibliographic aid:	
Approximate number of inquiries	= 100,000
Total cost per year	= $220,400
Cost per inquiry	= $2.20
Interlibrary loan	
Number of fulfilled requests	= 2899
Total cost of lending and borrowing system	= $21,340
Cost/fulfilled request	= $7.35
Number of seats	= 1631
Total cost per year	= $261,100
Cost per seat per year	= $160.00
Number of items repaired or rebound	= 2302
Total cost	= $34,768
Cost per item	= $15.10
Number of journal volumes bound	= 6,610
Total cost	= $53,403
Cost per journal	= $8.08

*Part of the total original cataloging costs pertains only to the cataloging of pamphlets in the Dewey Industrial Relations collection. The $11,620 deducted represents an estimate of these costs as reported in the time survey.

Appendix 5   Average Storage Costs*

Degree of Use	Access	Storage Type	Location	$Ft^2/$ Sec	Vol./Sec	Vol./Ft^2	Ft^2/Vol.	Unusable Area Factor	Gross Area Ft^2/Vol.
Infre-quent	Open	Conven-tional	On Campus	6.4	125	19.5	0.0512	1.15	0.0589
Moder-ate	Open	Conven-tional	On Campus	7.0	125	17.9	0.0560	1.20	0.0672
Heavy	Open	Conven-tional	On Campus	7.8	125	16.0	0.0624	1.25	0.0780
Moder-ate	Closed	Conven-tional	On Campus	6.4	125	19.5	0.0512	1.20	0.0614
Moder-ate	Closed	Com-pact	On Campus	6.4	244	38.1	0.0262	1.20	0.0314
Infre-quent	Open	Conven-tional	Off Campus	6.4	125	19.5	0.0512	1.15	0.0589
Moder-ate	Open	Conven-tional	Off Campus	7.0	125	17.9	0.0560	1.20	0.0672
Moder-ate	Closed	Conven-tional	Off Campus	6.4	125	19.5	0.0512	1.20	0.0614
Infre-quent	Closed	Com-pact	Off Campus	5.9	244	41.4	0.0242	1.15	0.0278
Moder-ate	Closed	Com-pact	Off Campus	6.4	244	38.1	0.0262	1.20	0.0314

*Capital investment repaid over 50 years.

Per Ft^2 Annual Mainte-nance Cost	Per Vol. Annual Mainte-nance Cost	At 4% Annual Interest on the Unpaid Principal				At 6% Annual Interest on the Unpaid Principal			
		Per Vol. Uniform Annual Storage Equip. Costs	Per Vol. Uniform Annual Con-struction Cost	Per Vol. Annual Land Costs	Per Vol. Annual Average Total Cost	Per Vol. Uniform Annual Storage Equip. Costs	Per Vol. Uniform Annual Con-struction Costs	Per Vol. Annual Land Costs	Per Vol. Annual Average Total Cost
$ .90	$.0530	$.0110	$.1042	$.0113	$.1795	$.0149	$.1420	$.0170	$.2269
1.25	.0840	.0125	.1189	.0129	.2283	.0171	.1620	.0194	.2825
1.50	.1170	.0145	.1380	.0150	.2845	.0198	.1881	.0225	.3474
1.25	.0768	.0114	.1086	.0118	.2086	.0156	.1480	.0177	.2581
1.25	.0393	.0088	.0555	.0060	.1096	.0120	.0757	.0090	.1360
.90	.0530	.0110	.0905	.0053	.1598	.0149	.1233	.0080	.1992
1.25	.0840	.0125	.1032	.0060	.2057	.0171	.1407	.0091	.2509
1.25	.0768	.0114	.0943	.0055	.1880	.0156	.1286	.0083	.2293
.60	.0167	.0078	.0324	.0025	.0594	.0106	.0441	.0038	.0752
1.25	.0393	.0088	.0482	.0028	.0991	.0120	.0658	.0042	.1213

Appendix 6 Data for Criteria Comparison

Years Old	Acquired up to	Total Circulations 1964–1967*	Total Books Removed	Percent Books Removed	Percent Circulations Lost
A. Acquisition Date					
25–34	1929	0	10	0 %	5.3%
15–24	1939	9	27	3.2	14.4
10–14	1949	42	66	14.8	35.0
5–9	1954	75	91	26.5	48.5
2–4	1959	162	130	57.2	69.1
1	1962	283	188	100.0	100.0
B. Publication Date					
25–34	1929	1	14	0 %	0 %
15–24	1939	16	35	5.7	18.8
10–14 / 5–9	1949 / 1954	59	77	21.0	41.2
2–4	1959	172	145	61.0	77.5
1	1962	282	187	100.0	100.0

1963 Circulation	Cumulative Number of Books	Cumulative Total Circulations 1964–1967	Percent Books Removed	Percent Circulations Lost
C. Circulation Date				
0	126	84	67.0%	30.0%
1	163	156	87.0	55.4
2	172	190	91.5	67.5
3	177	212	94.5	75.0
4	183	258	97.5	91.6
5	186	272	99.9	96.5
6	187	279	99.9	99.0
9	188	282	100.0	100.0

1963 Circulation	Cumulative Number of Books	Cumulative Total Circulations 1964 1967	Percent Books Removed	Percent Circulations Lost
D. Foreknowledge				
0	99	0	52.5%	0 %
1	130	31	69.1	11.5
2	154	79	82.0	28.9
3	166	115	88.3	42.0
4	174	147	92.6	53.6
5	176	157	93.6	57.4
6	176	157	93.6	57.4
7	178	171	94.7	62.4
8	183	211	97.5	77.1
9	185	229	98.5	83.8
10	185	229	98.5	83.8
11	186	240	99.0	87.8
12	186	240	99.0	87.8
13	186	240	99.0	87.8
14	186	240	99.0	87.8
15	186	240	99.0	87.8
16	188	272	100.0	100.0

*January 1964 through July 1967.

Appendix 7   Projected Students and Faculty at M.I.T.

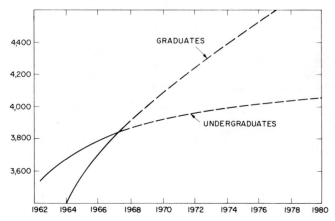

Figure 15.   Projected student enrollment at M.I.T.

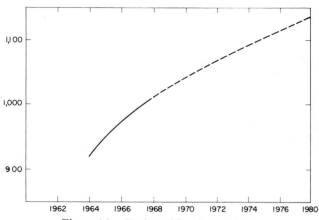

Figure 16.   Projected faculty at M.I.T.

86

Appendix 8 Departmental Library Alternatives*

Collection Description	A Center for International Studies	B Minimal Departmental	C Very Current Collection	D Extensive Collection	E Extensive Service
Example					
Total collection:					
(a) Journals	2000	2000	2000	4000	2000
(b) Books	3000	3000	3000	6000	3000
Purchases per year:					
(a) Journals	225	225	225	450	225
(b) Books	300	300	600	600	300
Circulation	Limited	Limited	Limited	Limited	Allowed
Seats	7-table	20-table	20-table	30-table	20-table
Cost categories:					
(a) Selection					
(b) Ordering					
(c) Preparation	$4400	$4400	$8800	$8800	$4400
(d) Cataloging					
(e) Purchasing					
(1) Journals	2000	2000	2000	4000	2000
(2) Books	2750	2750	5500	5500	2750
(f) Storage	520	520	520	1040	520
(g) Reference, information	2650	100	100	100	4000
(h) Circulation	250	100	100	100	3000
(i) Study spaces	800	3000	3000	4500	3000
TOTAL	$13,570	$12,870	$20,020	$24,040	$17,670

*Projected from current facilities and costs.

87

Appendix 9　Study-Reserve Alternatives

	Book Purchase	Xerox	Fiche Dupli- cation	Equip- ment	Person- nel	Floor Space	Seating
Microfiche							
Portable-readers	$75,000	$ 0	$54,000	$216,000	$170,000	$25,000	$196,000
Library-dorm readers							
(1:10 students)	75,000	0	54,000	36,000	170,000	25,000	196,000
(1:5 students)	75,000	0	54,000	72,000	170,000	25,000	196,000
(1:20 students)	75,000	0	54,000	18,000	170,000	25,000	196,000
(1:10 + 1:100 reader printers)	75,000	0	54,000	64,800	170,000	25,000	196,000
*Xerox**							
All article Commercial rates	75,000	138,000	0	0	170,000	25,000	196,000
Elastic demand	81,000	22,000	0	0	197,000	25,000	196,000
Inelastic demand	81,000	34,000	0	0	197,000	25,000	196,000
Conventional							
Present system	81,000	18,000	0	0	197,000	25,000	196,000
Departmental Libraries							
Supplement (10)	141,000	18,000	0	0	290,000	95,000	196,000
Replacement (10)	100,000	25,000	0	0	285,000	25,000	196,000
Additional copies (Low cost assumption)	113,400	36,000	0	0	200,000	28,000	196,000
(High cost)	263,700	54,000	0	0	200,000	28,000	196,000
Centralized reserve (say 25% overlap)	65,000	13,500	0	0	170,000	22,000	163,000

*Dewey and Student Center Xeroxing is estimated to be about two-thirds of the total Xeroxing budget for the library.

†Numbers in parentheses are the estimated percentages of seats "saved."

Total Cost with Current Seating	Total Cost with Probable Seating Effect†	Total Cost with Optimistic Seating Effect†	Total Cost with Probable Seating plus 25% Technological Price Changes
$736,000	$696,800 (20%)	$657,600 (40%)	$629,300
556,000	546,200 (5%)	497,200 (30%)	523,700
592,000	582,200 (5%)	533,200 (30%)	550,700
584,800	528,200 (5%)	479,200 (30%)	510,200
584,800	575,000 (5%)	526,000 (30%)	544,450
604,000	545,200 (30%)	506,000 (50%)	510,700
521,000	519,000 (1%)	501,400 (10%)	—
533,000	531,000 (1%)	507,400 (10%)	—
517,000	—	—	—
740,000	674,600 (33%)	642,000 (50%)	—
631,000	—	—	—
573,400	534,200 (20%)	495,000 (40%)	—
741,700	702,500 (20%)	663,300 (40%)	—
433,500	433,500 (1/6 Economy of Scale)	368,800 (1/3 Economy of Scale)	—

Appendix 10   Number and Price of U.S. Serials and Periodicals by Category Projected Through 1976 (Based on data from *Publisher's Weekly*).

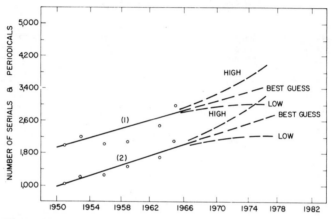

Figure 17.   Growth in U.S. serials and periodicals by category projected through 1976.   (1) All physical and natural sciences and all engineering; (2) All social sciences, business, finance, and history.

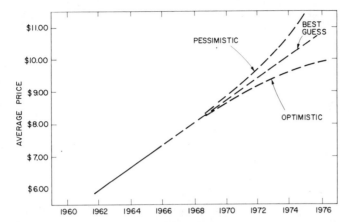

Figure 18.   Average price of U.S. periodicals projected through 1976. This average is computed from the individual average price of periodicals for 24 subject categories weighted by the proportion of periodicals published in that category.

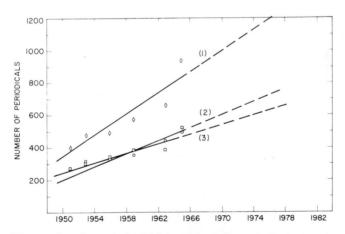

Figure 19.   Growth in U.S. serials and periodicals in the natural sciences and engineering projected through 1976. (1) Mathematics and natural sciences except chemistry and physics; (2) Chemistry and physics; (3) All engineering.

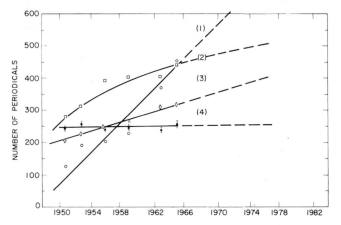

Figure 20.   Growth of U.S. periodicals and serials in the social sciences projected through 1976. (1) Management and economics; (2) Political science and international relations; (3) Sociology and anthropology; (4) Labor and industrial relations

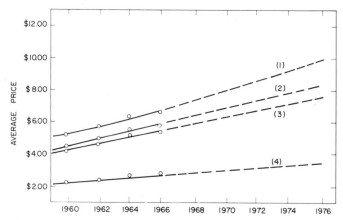

Figure 21.   Average price of U.S. periodicals by category projected through 1976. (1) Business and economics; (2) Political science; (3) Sociology and anthropology; (4) Labor and industrial relations.

Appendix 11   Duplicating Catalogs on Microform

	Initial Costs	Duplicating Costs per Copy	Cost to Each School if Divided Equally
A. Harvard plus M.I.T.	$490,000	$24,500	$257,250
B. M.I.T. plus Wellesley	85,000	4,250	44,625
C. M.I.T. plus Wellesley and 5 (1/2 million volume) libraries	210,000	10,250	38,785
D. M.I.T. plus Wellesley and Harvard	645,000	32,250	109,000

Appendix 12   Number and Price of U.S. Hardcover and Paperback Books by Category Projected Through 1976

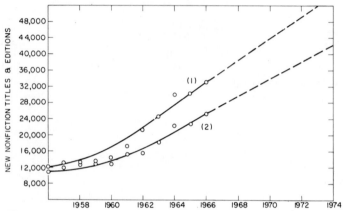

Figure 22. Annual number of new nonfiction titles and editions including imports (as listed in *Publishers' Weekly*) available in the U.S. projected through 1974. (1) Hardcover and paperback; (2) Hardcover only.

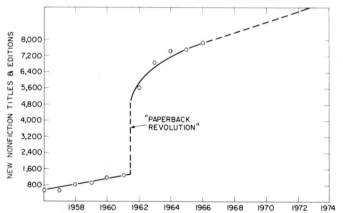

Figure 23. Annual number of new U.S. paperback nonfiction titles and editions (as listed in *Publishers' Weekly*) projected through 1974.

94

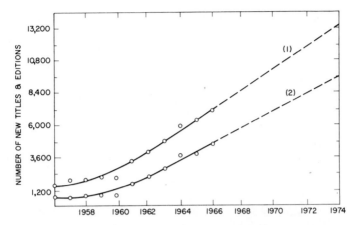

Figure 24.   Annual number of new U.S. hardcover and paperback titles and editions (as listed in *Publishers' Weekly*) by
category projected through 1974.   (1) Sociology, economics,
business, and history; (2) Sociology and economics.

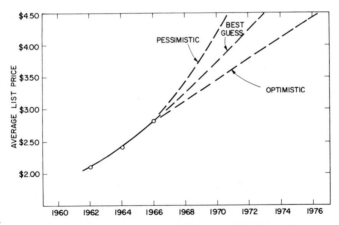

Figure 25.   Average list price of U.S. published trade paperback books projected through 1976. This average is computed
from the individual average list price of paperback books for
eighteen subject categories weighted by the proportion of new
paperback books published in that category.

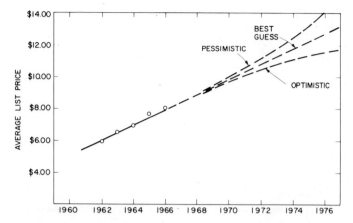

Figure 26. Average list price of U.S. published hardcover, trade-technical books projected through 1976. This average is computed from the individual average list price of books for nineteen subject categories weighted by the proportion of books published in that category.

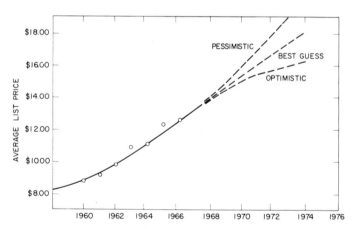

Figure 27. Average list price of U.S. published science and engineering books projected through 1976.

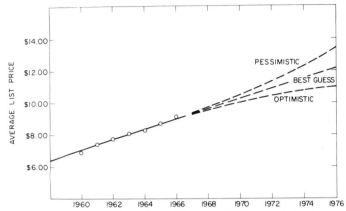

Figure 28.   Average list price of U.S. published social science books projected through 1976.   This average is derived from projected prices of books in economics, business, political science, sociology, and history, weighted by the relative number of new titles and editions in that field.

Appendix 13   Systems by Cost and Preference Ranks

System	Cost	Cost Rank	Preference Rank
Lower Xerox rates	$10,000	1.5*	1
LC messenger	10,000	1.5	2
Add reserve copies	50,000	6.5	3
Increase acquisitions—20%	160,000	10.5	4
Increase acquisitions—10%	80,000	8	5
Add reference	25,000	3.5	6
Expand seating	25,000	3.5	7
Increase access	30,000	5	8
Departmental libraries	160,000	10.5	9
All Xerox reserve	80,000	9	10
Expand seating—20%	50,000	6.5	11

*Where costs were tied, average ranks are indicated. The relationship between cost rank and preference rank is statistically insignificant using any ordinal significance measure.

Appendix 14 Association Between System Pairs*

	1†	2	3	4	5	6	7	8	9	10	11
1†	—	−1.00	.17	− .02	.20	.34	.14	− .14	.37	.33	.23
2	−1.00	—	.26	.34	.31	.66	.32	.55	.56	.37	.42
3	.17	.26	—	−1.00	−1.00	−1.00	− .19	.42	− .07	− .14	.30
4	− .02	.34	−1.00	—	−1.00	−1.00	.22	− .09	− .28	.03	.25
5	.20	.31	−1.00	−1.00	—	−1.00	.27	.57	.36	− .05	− .36
6	.34	.66	−1.00	−1.00	−1.00	—	.29	1.00	.52	.84	− .57
7	.14	.32	− .19	.22	.27	.29	—	.38	.67	.82	− .03
8	− .14	.55	.42	− .09	.57	1.00	.38	—	.47	.49	.31
9	.37	.56	− .07	− .28	.36	.52	.67	.47	—	− .32	0 .05
10	.33	.37	− .14	.03	− .05	.84	.62	.49	− .32	—	.29
11	.23	.42	.30	.25	− .36	− .57	− .03	.31	− .05	.29	—
12	− .33	− .29	− .40	− .27	.55	.04	.53	.16	.88	− .32	−1.00
13	0	0	0	0	0	0	0	0	0	0	0
14	0	0	0	0	0	0	0	0	0	0	0
15	− .07	− .18	− .52	.07	.20	−1.00	− .31	− .62	.47	.09	− .05
16	.22	.38	− .26	.09	− .07	−1.00	.70	.05	.70	.53	.12
17	.01	.37	.11	− .17	− .07	.36	.20	.49	− .53	0	.33
18	.12	− .03	− .13	− .12	− .20	.29	.47	− .09	− .09	.09	− .17
19	.01	− .23	− .17	− .16	.32	.47	.61	.63	− .17	.08	.10
20	.05	.31	.26	.10	.17	.56	.45	.43	− .30	.11	.29

*As measured by Q.
†Number of system from original questionnaire.

12	13	14	15	16	17	18	19	20
− .33	0	0	− .07	.22	.01	.12	.01	.05
− .29	0	0	− .18	.38	.37	− .03	− .23	.3
− .40	0	0	− .52	− .26	.11	− .13	− .17	.26
− .27	0	0	.07	.09	− .17	− .12	− .16	.10
.55	0	0	.20	− .07	− .07	− .20	− .32	.1
.04	0	0	− 1.00	− 1.00	.36	.29	.47	.56
.53	0	0	− .31	.70	.20	.47	.61	.45
.16	0	0	− .62	.05	.49	− .09	.63	.43
.88	0	0	.49	.70	− .53	− .09	− .17	− .36
− .32	0	0	.09	.53	0	.09	.08	.11
− 1.00	0	0	− .05	.12	.33	− .17	.10	.29
—	0	0	− .51	− .05	− .09	.26	.60	− .13
0	—	0	0	0	0	0	0	0
0	0	—	0	0	0	0	0	0
− .51	0	0	—	− .49	− .63	.15	− .50	− .10
− .05	0	0	− .49	—	− .90	− .31	− .48	.48
− .09	0	0	− .63	− .90	—	.31	.61	.14
.26	0	0	.15	− .31	.31	—	.89	.29
.60	0	0	− .50	− .48	.61	.89	—	.18
− .13	0	0	− .10	.48	.14	.29	.18	—

Bibliography

Ash, Lee. *Yale's Selective Book Retirement Program.* New York: Shoe String Press, 1963.

Arrow, Kenneth J. *Social Choice and Individual Values.* New York: John Wiley & Sons, Inc., 1951.

Behling, Orlando, and Kermit Cudd. "A Library Looks at Itself." *College and Research Libraries*, November 1967.

Bush, G. C., H. P. Galliher, and Philip M. Morse, "Attendance and Use of the Science Library at M.I.T." *American Documentation*, Vol. VII, No. 2, pp. 87–109.

Dorfman, Robert (ed.). *Measuring Benefits of Government Investments.* Washington, D.C.: The Brookings Institution, 1965.

Downs, Anthony. *An Economic Theory of Democracy.* New York: Harper & Row Publishers, 1957.

Gipson, John S. "'Total Cost' of Acquisitions in a Community College." *College and Research Libraries*, July 1967.

Grant, Eugene L., and W. Grant Jerson. *Principles of Engineering Economy.* New York: The Ronald Press Company, 1964 (first edition, 1930).

Hitch, Charles, and Roland N. McKean. *The Economics of Defense in the Nuclear Age.* Cambridge, Mass.: Harvard University Press, 1960.

Information Systems Office. *Project MARC.* Washington, D.C.: Library of Congress, 1967.

Jain, A. K. "Sampling and Short-Period Usage in the Purdue Library." *College and Research Libraries*, May 1966.

Kendall, Willmoore, and George W. Carey. "The 'Intensity' Problem and Democratic Theory." *American Political Science Review*, Vol. LXII (March 1968), pp. 5–24.

Library of Congress. *Annual Report of the Librarian of Congress, 1966,* Washington, D.C., 1967.

Lister, Winston C. *Least Cost Decision Rules for the Selection of Library Materials for Compact Storage.* Ph.D. Thesis, Purdue University, 1967.

McKean, Roland N. *Efficiency in Government through Systems Analysis: With Emphasis on Water Resources Development.* New York: John Wiley & Sons, Inc., 1958.

Metcalf, Keyes D. *Planning Academic and Research Library Buildings.* New York: McGraw-Hill Publishing Company, Inc., 1965.

Morse, Philip M. *Probabilistic Models for Library Operations.* Lecture delivered at midwinter meeting of Association of Research Libraries, Chicago, Illinois, January 26, 1964.

Morse, Philip M. *A Systems Approach to Library Effectiveness.* Cambridge, Mass.: The M.I.T. Press, 1968.

Novick, David. *Program Budgeting.* Cambridge, Mass.: Harvard University Press, 1965.

Overhage, Carl F. J., and R. Joyce Harmon. *INTREX: The Report of a Planning Conference on Information Transfer Experiments.* Cambridge, Mass.: The M.I.T. Press, 1965.

Quade, E. S. (ed.) *Analyses for Military Decisions.* Chicago: Rand-McNally & Company, 1965.

Scherer, Frederic M. "Government Research and Development Programs," in Robert Dorfman (ed.) *Measuring Benefits of Government Investments.* Washington, D.C.: The Brookings Institution, 1965.

Sherwood, Thomas K. (Chairman). "Report of Ad Hoc Committee on Long-Range Planning for the Libraries," M.I.T., 1962.

Simon, Julian L. "How Many Books Should be Stored Where? An Economic Analysis." *College and Research Libraries*, March 1967.

Sommer, Robert, and Peggy Peterson. "Study Carrels Re-examined." *College and Research Libraries*, July 1967.

Wessel, C. J. *Criteria for Evaluating the Effectiveness of Library Operations and Services: Phase I—Literature Search and State of the Art.* Washington, D.C.: John J. Thompson, 1967.

Index

Access, closed, 7, 9
  open, 7, 9
  to other collections, 40
Acquisition, common, 45
  benefit evaluation of, 58–67
Additional copies, cataloging of, 27
  and circulation periods, 27
  costs, 27
  benefit evaluation of, 58, 63, 66
A fortiori arguments, 38
Aisle width, 7, 8
Arrow, Kenneth J., 48, 61
Augmented catalog, 36

Benefit measure, desirable characteristics
  of, 46–48
Benefit questionnaire. *See* Benefit survey
Benefits, level of, 13, 15, 18, 27, 36, 43,
  44, 46–48
  loss in, 14, 22, 38, 39, 43, 44
  social, 27
  survey of. *See* Benefit survey
Benefit survey, 49–55
  problems of, 49, 55–58
  response patterns of, 61–63
  subgroup analysis of, 63–67
Bookstore, incorporation with library, 1,
  23, 25, 62
Book usage, 15–17, 43, 72, 73
Broadcast Music, Inc. (BMI), 25 n
Browsing, 13–15, 46
Budget, of M.I.T. libraries, 3–6, 39, 47,
  48, 67
Budget, program. *See* Program budget

Capital recovery factor, 12, 18
Carrels, 28, 33, 34
Catalog, microstrip, 41
  on-line computerized, 41

Cataloging, classifying, 36
  costs, 5, 36
  limited, 36, 37
  original, 37
  temporary, 37, 38
Centralization, of study-reserve system,
  27
  benefit evaluation of, 58, 60, 61, 64, 65
Central Processing and Handling Services, 3
Circulation control, 27, 29
Circulation probability density functions, 43
Conclusions, on book storage, 21, 22, 68,
  69
  on cataloging, 70, 72
  on measuring benefits, 71
  on microform storage, 21, 22, 69
  on ordering, 39, 71
  on program budgeting, 68
  on retrieval, 40, 71
  on selection, 41, 43, 70, 71
  on the study-reserve system, 29–32, 69,
  70, 72
Copyright law, as pertains to libraries,
  25
Cost-benefit analysis, *v*
Cost-effectiveness, 19, 46, 47
Costs, capital, 4, 11, 12
  of circulations, 5, 14
  construction, 11
Costs, interest, 12
  land, 11
Costs, maintenance, 11
  microform storage, 21
  motorized retrieval, 19, 21
Costs, personnel, 3, 36
Costs, storage, 5, 13–15, 22
  storage equipment, 12
Costs, supplies, 4, 6
  weeding, 17, 18
Criteria, weeding, 15–19

Decentralization, costs, 29
   benefit evaluation of, 58, 60, 63, 65
   of study-reserve system, 29
Decentralized retrieval, 21
Departmental libraries, 29, 56
   benefit evaluation of, 58, 60, 63, 65
   costs, 29
Departmental reading rooms, 29, 56
Departments, cataloging, 3, 36
   acquisitions, 3
   circulation, 3
Dewey Decimal System, 15, 18
Dewey library, 3, 17, 18, 28
   survey, 26
Divisional libraries, 3
Domination, of one alternative by another, 17, 21, 26, 44

Economies of scale, 27
Economies, external, 21, 41
Effectiveness, vs. efficiency, 46, 47
Efficiency, vs. effectiveness, 46, 47

Faculty, preferences of, 64, 65
Federal City College, 1
Fringe benefits, 3

General administration, 3
Graduate students, preference of, 62

Hayden library, 3, 6
Hermann building, 11. *See also* Dewey
   library

Incommensurables, measuring, 47–49
Interlibrary loan, as alternative to purchasing, 40, 43
   in combination with direct messenger
   service, 40, 62, 64, 65
   reaction time, 40
Intransitivities, of paired comparisons,
   49

Journals, and departmental reading
   rooms, 63
   on microfilm, 39
   number of, 39
   prices of, 39
   and Xerox, 26

Kendall's Q measure, 61

Library of Congress, cataloging, 36–38
   Chief Legal Counsel, 25 n
Library of Congress messenger service,
   costs, 40
   benefit evaluation of, 58, 60, 64
Limited cataloging, 36
   savings from, 36
   benefit evaluation of, 58, 61–64
Lindgren library, 27, 28
Linear programming, 33, 34
Lister, Winston C., 19 n
Long-range planning, 2, 24

Maintenance, costs, 11
Materials appropriation, 39
Messenger service, cost, 40
   in combination with interlibrary loan,
   40
Metcalf, Keyes D., 7, 9
Microfiche readers, in dormitories and
   libraries, 26, 27
   portable, 26
   and user behavior, 26, 27
Microfiche systems, costs, 26, 27
Microform readers, 21, 22, 26, 27
Microform storage, costs, 21, 22
Microstrip catalog, costs, 41
Missions, of M.I.T. libraries, 2
M.I.T. Center for International Studies,
   v
M.I.T. collection, standardization of, 14
M.I.T. community, 47, 48, 57, 58, 67
M.I.T. Comptroller's Office, 3 n
M.I.T. Director of Libraries, v, 49
M.I.T. dormitories, 23, 26, 47
M.I.T. library, perceived purposes of,
   66, 67
M.I.T. library budget, 3–6, 39, 47, 48, 67
M.I.T. Operations Office, 11
M.I.T. Superintendent's Office, 4, 10
Morse, Phillip M., 17 n, 43 n, 46 n

Neutral good, 56 n
Novick, David, 46 n

Objectives of M.I.T. libraries, 1, 2, 23
Ordering, alternatives, 39
   journals on microfilm, 39
Outside use orientation, 61, 62
Overhead, on M.I.T. libraries, 3

Paperbacks, use of, 27, 63, 67
Present value, 40

Personal discount rate, 48
Personnel, costs, 3, 36
Problem formulation, in systems analysis, 1
Program budget, *vi*, 3–6, 23, 24, 35
Project INTREX, 36
Project MARC, 38, 39
Proofreading, of catalog cards, 36

Range length, 7, 8
Rationality, in benefit survey, 56
Reference staff, benefit evaluation of, 58, 61, 62, 64, 65, 67
Required reading, 23, 24, 26, 27
Research orientation, 61–63
Research requirements, alternatives for, 35
Retrieval systems, extra-M.I.T., 40
from remote storage, 19, 21

Savings, by compact storage, accumulated, 19
annual, 14, 15
Seating, benefit evaluation of, 58–60, 65, 66
costs, 28
demand for, 24–27
in present study-reserve system, 24
requirements, 24–27
in research libraries, 33
optimal accommodations, 33, 34
uncertainty in use of, 24–27
Selection, alternatives, 44
optimal, 43, 44
policies, 41–43
Serendipity, 47
Serials, number of, 39
price of, 39
Shelving, mechanical, 9, 10
Scherer, Frederic M., 48
Significant uses, as benefit measure, 43, 44, 46
Social welfare, 47–49
Social welfare function, 49, 61
Stacks, capacity, 9, 10
floorplan, 8
Storage, alternatives, 13
benefit evaluation of, 58, 60, 64, 65
compact, 9, 10, 13–15, 22
conventional, 9, 13, 14
microform, 21, 22
policies, 7, 13
total costs of, 13, 20
Student Center, 3, 27, 28

Study-reserve system, 23–32
alternatives, 30–32
centralization of, 27
objectives, 23
Suboptimization, in seating accommodations, 33, 34
in weeding, 15–19
Superior good, 56 n
Supplies, costs, 4, 6
Survey, of benefits. *See* Benefit survey
Survey research, 48, 49
Systematic policy analysis, *v. See also* Systems analysis
Systems analysis, 1, 34

Technical Information Project (T.I.P.), 4
Telephone hot-line, 41
Television, closed circuit, 41
Temporary cataloging, savings from, 38
Time survey, personnel, 3
Title IIC, 37
Trade-offs, *vi*, 44, 48, 49

Uncertainty, in prices, 17, 18, 39, 41
in technology, *v*, 41
in use of seating, 24–27
in user behavior, 25, 73
Undergraduates, preferences of, 64
Uniform annual costs, 3, 11, 12
Unusable area factor (UAF), 8
Unusable area, in libraries, 8
Use encouragement, 1, 47

Volume equivalents, 14

Weeding, criteria, 15–17
costs, 17, 18
optimal decision rules for, 19
Wellesley, common acquisition with, 45
transportation system, 21

Xerox, all-Xerox reserve, 25
benefit evaluation of, 58, 59, 61, 63–65
demand curve for, 25
effect on circulation of journals, 26
effect on seating demand, 25, 26
pricing of, 25, 26

Yale Compact Storage Study, 9
Yale's Selective Book Retirement Program, 9, 12 n